Gov Geeks

THE GOV GEEKS GUIDE TO

GOVERNMENT RESUMES

JAVIER LOPEZ, MSA, PCC
KAREN LOPEZ, BS

WHAT THE GOV GEEKDOM IS SAYING...

"The Gov Geeks, Javier and Karen, have been phenomenal partners in my effort to find career fulfillment. From career coaching to professional development, The Gov Geeks have helped me discover a new passion for my career in a meaningful and GRAND way."

— Rosemary Hill

"Career coaching has helped me refine my professional aspirations and what I want from my role as a public servant. More than a standard resume writing service, Javier and The Gov Geeks placed a premium on supporting me in my journey to find meaningful work that helps others. I appreciate our time together and am excited to embrace my bright future serving the American people."

— James Harris

"*When it comes to improving your career satisfaction in government, Javier is the best. Imagine having your superhero help you navigate the Federal job market and have a fulfilling career in any government agency.* "

— John Neral

"*The Gov Geeks changed my life! Their passion for people and commitment to helping public servants reach career fulfillment is unmatched. As a coach, Javier helped me to discover professional possibilities that aligned with my passions. I now feel empowered to surpass my career goals and find real happiness in my work.*"

— Ashley Hill

"*I highly recommend Javier and The Gov Geeks for their skill in professional career development. Javier has helped me navigate the federal career application process with excellent results. With his coaching, I feel confident navigating USAJOBS and have even been referred for several positions.*"

— Patricia Doyle

THE GOV GEEKS GUIDE TO

GOVERNMENT RESUMES

LiveLifeHappy
Publishing

LiveLife**Happy**
Publishing

Library of Congress Cataloging-in-Publication Data
Lopez, Javier and Lopez, Karen
The Gov Geeks Guide to Resumes\ Javier Lopez and Karen Lopez
1. Nonfiction > Business & Economics > Careers > Job Hunting
2. Nonfiction > Business & Economics > Mentoring & Coaching
978-1-990461-03-3
LLH Publishing House
1st Printing: August 2021. Printed in The USA
2nd Printing: March 2023. Printed in The USA
Cover Photo Credit: Arianna Lopez
Proof-reader & Editor: Lindy Bailey

Publisher's Note & Author DISCLAIMER

This publication is designed to provide accurate and authoritative information concerning the subject matter covered. It is sold to understand that the publisher and author are not engaging in or rendering any psychological, medical or other professional services. If expert assistance or counseling is needed, seek the services of a competent medical professional. For immediate support, call your local crisis line. BE WELL.

Contents

DEDICATION

To Arianna and Kessia

Thank you for filling our lives with love, joy, and purpose.

To our fellow public servants

Thank you for your service!

PREFACE

You have taken your first step into a larger world! Welcome to the first book in The Gov Geeks career management series! Redesigned with a new structure that is aligned across the series, this book will help you find a fulfilling career with the federal government.

Public service is a rewarding and noble career with opportunities you can't get anywhere else. You may be reading this because you have an interest in becoming a public servant or a desire to get ahead in government. Either way – The Gov Geeks are here to help!

In the following pages, you will find straightforward and easy to apply strategies from experts and fellow public servants written in an engaging and fun way - even the formatting was designed to be easy to use. We included the key Topics covered at the start of each chapter for your quick reference. At the close of each chapter, we included a notes and reflections section with helpful questions for you to consider as you build your resume. Feel free to write in your book (yup, we just saw our high school English teacher cringe in our minds too). We designed this as a guide to offer you value.

As executives with over 40 years of shared public service experience, as well as nearly 20 in academia, insights from The Gov Geeks are of particular value. We are pleased to share many of them with you in this book. In our minds, the further this information is distributed, the more qualified applicants can excel in careers that serve our country. In this way, we all benefit.

Thank you for inviting us along your journey. We look forward to seeing where your career takes you!

Javier Lopez, MSA, PCC
Geek in Chief | Government Career Coach

Karen Lopez, BA
Executive Director | Government Career Coach

A NOTE ON THE 2ND EDITION

Karen and I have been overwhelmed by the warm response we received from the first edition. We heard from educators, professional societies, hiring managers, and countless public servants who found value in the first edition. A reliable resource that has helped transform lives and stay relevant on the book has been a tremendous success. So we took it upon ourselves to add even more resources to it and kick off a book series as well!

In this edition and in the series, you'll find recommendations for further career research, expanded self-reflection activities to help you zero in on your interests, and connections to resources to help you make the most of your career in public service. Each has been carefully crafted with you in mind. We hope you enjoy this edition as well as the growing book series and look forward to hearing from you!

— Javier and Karen

ABOUT THIS BOOK SERIES

ABOUT THIS BOOK

The features in this book have been designed to empower you with actionable content. This isn't a standard workbook, career text, or common counseling text found on the shelves of decision-makers. The pages in this guide are meant to be written in, reflected upon, and revisited as often as needed. This is your tool to build the life you want. It's a guide to reaching your aspirations and worthy of all your years of study, dreaming, and looking to the horizon for a future just out of reach. We encourage you to embrace the lessons and apply them with vigor. Your best deserves nothing less.

The tone has been carefully crafted to be easy going, conversational, and fun! We have seen too many career resources come across as stuffy or out of touch. Your career should reflect your unique blend of interests and cares. In our eyes, the materials you use to support your growth should reflect that. So feel free to relax and take in the content. We're here to support you and look forward to sharing solid interview strategies and a few laughs too.

••• CONNECT THE DOTS •••

Direct and open-ended questions designed to offer you the opportunity to reflect and design your fate. Make meaning of what you read by internalizing it and applying your own insights. In this way, you'll be empowered to take the content in this book and combine it with your own knowledge to develop previously unrealized insights. From there, you can apply those insights to determine the best strategy for your career development. This is your earned wisdom and the real value this book presents you. As the below diagram illustrates, it's not the data or information in this book that is of value, it is the combination of them that makes the concepts life changing.

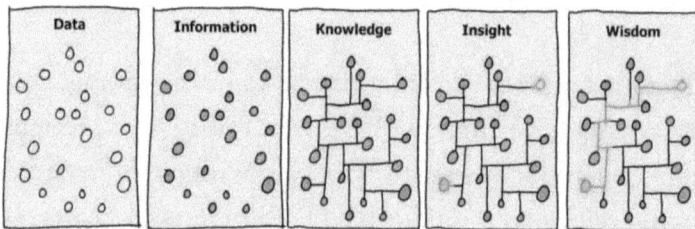

Track your thoughts throughout the book and revisit the questions to develop your interview approach. Connect with the concepts and give yourself the opportunity to find depth to your perspectives.

STRUCTURE

This book is a guide to aid in your interview preparation efforts. Separate from a textbook with an abundance of knowledge to memorize or a technical reference list to consult for periodic use, it is a tool to support your reflection and growth. As famous American educator John Dewey reminds us, we do not learn from experience… we learn from reflecting on experience (Dewey, 1933).

We encourage you to use the insights as you plan your interview approaches and develop a sense of your values for the potential position. Maybe you'll find that what you thought you valued doesn't align with your expectations. Perhaps you'll see the job opportunity truly fits with your career ambitions but for different reasons than you initially suspected. It's much better to find these answers out now instead of six months into a job that you only realize that you really don't like!

INSIDER'S TIPS

This guide is a compilation of many helpful tips and strategies, but it is not the total sum of what is available to you. We added these sections to help you identify other sources to consider and materials to prepare you for your interviews. Direct citations considered from the lens of government work, you'll be given the opportunity to learn from industry experts and thought leaders in a meaningful way. Take a moment to consider the varied perspectives and embrace what is possible. You may come to realize that there are more aspects of your career and interview preparation than you anticipated.

NOTES AND REFLECTIONS

Thoughtful questions guide our growth and development. As coaches and human capital experts, we have seen the value of embracing reflection as a developmental tool. We highly encourage you to reflect on the questions to give yourself a moment to manage the chaos of the job hunt and the pressures of the job interview. Sort through the meaning of the questions, not just answer them. Connecting the book's content with your experiences and considering an alternative perspective is your gateway to growth and career fulfillment.

CHAPTER 1:

BASICS WORTH REPEATING

Some basic resume writing concepts will be familiar to you but that doesn't mean they're worth skipping over. In fact, you may know of them because of how critical they are to a solid career strategy. That said, there are some nuances that will be of value to you – so let's dive in!

TOPICS COVERED:
- Your email address matters
- Format for the systems
- Beware the acronyms

YOUR EMAIL ADDRESS MATTERS

More often than not we see email addresses that are simply not professional. This is a known concept but even the most experienced candidates run into this challenge. The following tips and pointers will help you manage any potential concerns. Be mindful of being in the 'I don't have that issue' camp. You may just learn that your email address is not the most professional option available!

Make sure that it is something appropriate for the audience that is receiving the information. If you were applying for executive positions, perhaps it's not ideal to use your existing college address. Also, if you're applying for a federal job, do not use your current government job email address. This way you're focusing more on the position that you are aiming for, as opposed to demonstrating the one that you have right now.

It is worth repeating: make sure that your email address is professional sounding. A good old first name dot last name @ Gmail or Hotmail will work well.

Alternatively, you can decide to create an email address specifically for your campaign. This way, you can make sure that you are monitoring and sending the right messages to the right individuals using the right tone. You can also create your own signature block for each of these. The importance of this is to present yourself as the most professional individual possible. As a bonus, using a special email address can limit the amount of junk or personal messages you have to wade through to get to your new job messages.

••• CONNECT THE DOTS •••

Consider your email address. Do you feel it could be improved upon or would you like to create a new one specific to your job search? Take a moment to see what's available and write down a few options here.

_____

_____

_____

_____

_____

_____

_____

_____

_____

_____

_____

_____

_____

_____

_____

_____

_____

_____

FORMAT FOR THE SYSTEMS

Next, make sure that your resume is formatted appropriately. Agencies use different types of technology to manage their workload. These are Applicant Tracking Systems or ATSs. Some agencies and organizations use these a little bit more closely than others, but the large theme is still the same. The system has to be able to read the information that you are presenting. With this said, make sure that your resume can be read by these programs. What do we mean by this? First, make sure that you are using one-inch margins, and that the text is very plain and very simple. Next, don't use a whole lot of extra unique or special character fonts that can't be translated well into word or notepad documents. Also, don't use any pictures or any loud types of fonts or formatting that makes it more challenging to read. The systems need to recognize the characters in order to manage your information.

Remember, government resumes don't have to be limited to one page. In our experience, the successful applicant can have a resume anywhere from two, three, and even up to five pages long. Make sure that the formatting looks good, not only for the systems, but for the readers as well. Make it engaging; something that human resource professionals and hiring managers would like to read.

If your resume is a whole lot of text and it's just completely filled page to page, or if there are tons of pictures all over, it won't be something that they will want to take the time to look at. So, make sure that it's formatted correctly. Give yourself the best shot possible.

••• CONNECT THE DOTS •••

After considering this section, what areas could be improved upon? Take this opportunity to write down a few planned activities you feel are important to address.

_____
_____
_____
_____
_____
_____
_____
_____
_____
_____
_____
_____
_____
_____
_____
_____
_____
_____

BEWARE OF THE ACRONYMS

Lastly, number three, make sure to address all of the acronyms. Working in government is fun because it's basically alphabet soup. There's an acronym for almost everything. The positions, the organizations, the titles, addresses - the list goes on and on - but they are also unique to that individual agency or organization.

So, for the reader, make sure you spell out what those acronyms are. When and where to do this, you ask? Right at the top. You should structure your resume with a summary in the beginning along with your background information. Spell out the acronyms there. Then, later on when you're describing your individual qualifications from your positions, spell out the acronyms again. This way the reader isn't going back and forth from the beginning to your experience area to try to figure out what the acronyms are. The more convenient you make it, the easier it will be for them to want to recommend you for the next round of review.

Also, look for different acronyms that they are interested in. For instance, if you're applying for financial jobs, put in the financial systems that you're working with. If it's acquisition jobs, same thing, use those acquisition acronyms. If you're a part of the intelligence community, use the acronyms that are used there as well. You want to convey that you have the expertise that they are looking for in a new hire. Show them you speak their language and they'll be more inclined to consider you for the role.

There you have it. Three basic tips worth repeating to help get your resume into shape. Let's jump into the next topic!

••• CONNECT THE DOTS •••

Workplace and professional acronyms are all over the place. It may help us to create communities and quickly convey an understanding of something but it can restrict access for others. What are your acronyms to be aware of in your writing?

_____

_____

_____

_____

_____

_____

_____

_____

_____

_____

_____

_____

_____

_____

_____

_____

NOTES AND REFLECTIONS

Does your email address need an update? List some potential replacements here.

_____

_____

_____

_____

_____

_____

_____

Look at your resume. What Applicant Tracking System (ATS) updates can you make?

_____

_____

_____

_____

_____

_____

_____

Acronym tracker. Take a moment to capture key acronyms here.

_____

_____

_____

_____

_____

_____

_____

Think of the best thing this resume can do for you. Why is this important to you?

_____

_____

_____

_____

_____

_____

_____

INSIDER'S TIP

Knowing where you're going and why can help you to feel empowered and in control of your career journey. As we've seen it no small amount of frustration comes from ambiguity in your professional life. The idea of believing that if you work hard enough, someone will come along to tap you on the shoulder to offer you the next promotion or big project only to feel isolated and overlooked is challenging and a significant factor in why clients and colleagues seek us out for coaching. Thankfully there's something that can be done about that feeling.

We're happy to refer you to Kanika Tolver. The CEO and founder of Career Rehab, LLC, Kanika has a wealth of knowledge to share with each of us. She joined us for an episode on our podcast, Gov Geeks Assemble, and has an awesome book that discusses (among many other great things) a career rehab blueprint. Take a moment to order your copy and begin orienting yourself toward meaningful success in your career!

Tolver, K. (2020). *Career rehab: Rebuild your personal brand and rethink the way you work.* Entrepreneur Press.

CHAPTER 2:

STRUCTURE MATTERS

We have seen all sorts of formats and styles of resumes over the years. While it's good to express individuality and attempt to stand out from the application crowd, using the wrong structure can cause your resume to sink to the bottom of the pile instead of rising to the top. Give yourself the best possible chance to be approved by HR practitioners and selecting officials alike with these strategies!

TOPICS COVERED:
- Structure matters
- Bucket your resume by desirable skill areas
- Include key accomplishments

STRUCTURE MATTERS

At the risk of sounding redundant, it's important to state the obvious: structure matters. We want to share three things with you regarding the structure of your resume. Number one, as far as the structure goes, make sure you're including relevant information. Number two, bucket your experiences by desirable skill areas. Lastly, number three, include key accomplishments. Let us explain a little bit about what we're talking about.

First, include relevant information. You want to make sure that you are providing the information that they actually care about. It may be something that you had a great experience with in the past, or that you are great at what you're doing now. But what you are looking to do is to demonstrate how great you are at what they are looking for by structuring your content. It's not ideal for you to say, "I was great at doing this stuff back then," but rather, "This is how I can do the stuff that you're interested in." Make it about them. Make sure the hiring manager gets a good understanding that you are the person to do the work that is needed. As you build your resume, you'll see the trends and patterns across all of your previous experiences that relate to those areas of interest. Then, you can say that you have X years of experience in the subjects they care about. You can also say that you have worked across all areas of that type of work. Having a person on staff that has seen the work at all levels is a great thing for an organization to have available to them.

To identify what relevant information to include, look at the job duties and description of your target positions. They'll lay them out pretty clearly. Also look at the organization's website to get a good understanding about what it is that they're looking for from the person in this role. Now, I know you might be saying to yourself, "This is a lot! Will I have to do this for every single job that I apply for? There are so many jobs out there, how can I possibly find the time to create a new resume for each one?"

The thing to focus on is the patterns that you are seeing. Every time you're looking at job announcements, whether you're looking at USAJOBS, Monster, or one of the many other job sites out there, identify what patterns and trends you're seeing. For instance, are agencies looking for data analysis, writing, or communication skills? What are the key qualification factors that they are looking for? Once you know what those qualifications are, which you will find by doing some research - then you will know those are the things to really focus on in your resume. Making your resume relevant allows you to stay very marketable. This aspect alone is huge. We can't tell you how often this goes overlooked by resume writers. Don't try to fit an old resume with irrelevant experience into a job application. Demonstrate what they are looking for and you'll be well on your way!

••• CONNECT THE DOTS •••

What job duties have you seen pop up often in your career search? Pay close attention to action verbs you see and subject areas. Take a moment to jot down a few of the key items here.

_____

_____

_____

_____

_____

_____

_____

_____

_____

_____

_____

_____

_____

_____

_____

_____

_____

_____

_____

BUCKET YOUR RESUME BY DESIRABLE SKILL AREAS

A lot of times as we are working with clients we see that they put in just all sorts of information, and it seems very much scattered. While it may seem helpful to throw as much as you can into a resume just in case it may fit their needs, the truth is that it represents you as a person with a lot of experiences not related to the work of the target job. The hiring manager shouldn't have to hunt through your resume to see if they find something relevant. Think of a grocery store. You know where everything is based on neat isles of goods with labels and easy to navigate floor plans. Your resume should be the same. Make it easy for them. Help them help you… we think this was in a movie… show me the money!!

What you want to do is to align your experiences directly towards what they're looking for in an applicant. One of the best ways to do this is to bucket your experiences by those desirable skill areas.

Here's what we mean. Earlier we mentioned including relevant information. These relevant information areas could be information analysis, research and evaluation, communication skills, collaboration, whatever. Those are the bucketed areas. Quite simply start a new line with each of the areas relevant to you as a subheading in bold (and actually put the word in a bold font for effect) and then describe the experience that you have in each area. As a person is reading the resume they can quickly see that you have the key skills that they are looking for in each of the different positions that you've held. You're demonstrating that you have the qualifications to do the work that they are looking for. You are tailoring your resume to the specific job qualifications that you need. This strategy alone can yield such great results in your job search!

Believe it or not, this is an appropriate thing to do if you are entry-level, if you are a mid-level, or if you are an executive. It works across all levels in your career. The hiring manager is looking directly at each of these areas. As your career changes, those buckets will change as well, but your resume will stay up to date because you are ensuring you are writing to what hiring managers are looking for. Pretty great, right?

One last bonus with this approach: it makes it easy to skim through. We all know how quickly managers read through resumes. They have a lot going on, which is why they're hiring someone to help them out. Creating easy to follow buckets allows them to quickly scan for what they're looking for and get a good sense of a person's fit for the position. Structuring your resume in an easy-to-read pattern really cuts down on the time needed to review applicants and helps your resume float to the top of the pile.

••• **CONNECT THE DOTS** •••

It's all about the buckets. Hiring managers and human resources staff alike can see your qualifications easily when you use these. Help them see what you have to offer quickly rather than leaving it up to them to guess if you're the right fit. What buckets do you feel you need to share?

_____

_____

_____

_____

_____

_____

_____

_____

_____

_____

_____

_____

_____

_____

_____

INCLUDE KEY ACCOMPLISHMENTS

In each of the sections of your job experiences, you are writing to those buckets. Directly below these you can create another section, simply labeled: "key accomplishments" or "select key accomplishments." Then, have a quick bulleted list of some of those big successes. This is where you can describe some of the biggest impacts that you've had in your organizations. Make them high-impact statements. Write them to show how much you reduced, increased, performed, etc. Numbers are always a good way to go. For instance, by what percentage did you increase productivity or sales? By what percentage did you decrease operational risk? Think about some good ways of describing the work that you have done. Demonstrate the impact that you've had on the organization. It should be really quick, but at the same time should illustrate that you have the skills needed and relevant experiences to do the job that the hiring managers are looking for you to do. It's all about these hiring officials. The more that you can structure your resume around their needs, the better off you'll be. They should look at your resume and think: "Whoa – it would be great to have that done here. This is exactly the kind of qualifications I need to get this job done."

In this chapter, we've talked about three areas for structuring your resume. Number one: make sure you include relevant information. Number two: make sure you are bucketing them by desirable skill areas. And lastly, number three: include key accomplishments in your write-ups as well. When you start building all of these together, your resume will be even stronger. Remember, structure matters!

You've done the work already. You have these experiences. Now make sure your resume reflects your talents and qualifications. With a little practice and some careful consideration, your resume will shine. Think of it this way: the more you invest in your resume, the greater your career growth will be. How badly do you want that promotion or dream job? How many years have you worked through school, challenging bosses, and time away from family to gain these experiences? Odds are, you've worked your tail off to get to this point. Make sure you give yourself all the credit you deserve for those long hours. Your professional dreams and aspirations are right there for the taking. Go for it!

••• **CONNECT THE DOTS** •••

Think of the big ticket items you've been involved with. What was your role and how did it make a difference for the organization? Take a moment to write down a few of them below and where you can look to find more to include.

_____

_____

_____

_____

_____

_____

_____

_____

_____

_____

_____

_____

_____

_____

_____

_____

_____

_____

NOTES AND REFLECTIONS

How can you find what hiring managers are looking for? What do you need to include more of?

_____

_____

_____

_____

_____

_____

_____

What skills are needed for your target career? Where have you developed them in your career? Now, add up the years of experience you've earned 😄

_____

_____

_____

_____

_____

_____

_____

Consider your past roles. What would you list as your key accomplishments for each?

_____

_____

_____

_____

_____

_____

_____

INSIDER'S TIP

Documenting your accomplishments may take a bit of time. After running from task to task, the great victories start to look like business as usual. Plus, taking the time to capture all of your work throughout the year can be a challenge in itself. So much so that compiling a list of them can start to feel like a chore - and that's when you can re-member all of them! We realize this can be a task especially if you're squeezing resume writing into your already crowded schedule. But, it is worth-while and there are other tools at your disposal.

The Partnership for Public Service has developed a *Public Service Leadership 360 Assessment* tool to help leaders keep a pulse on their skills and com-petencies and those needed to lead government. A tremendous way to utilize part of your training and development dollars and nurture your professional development, the tool can help you accomplish wonders in your career and capture noteworthy success for your resume at the same time.

Partnership for Public Service. (n.d.). *Tools*. Public service leadership institute. Retrieved March 10, 2023, from https://ourpublicservice.org

CHAPTER 3:

THE STAR APPROACH

A frequent challenge we see as career coaches and resume professionals is the use of simple and incomplete bullets to describe work experiences. We get it. We've all been told to keep your resume to a page so we limit the amount of content. Often simply copying and pasting the job duties from our previous role. While this strategy may work in certain industries, it is not the best approach to get a position in the federal government. Your resume needs to demonstrate that you have the qualifications necessary to do the work and the competencies to make an impact in the organization. Hiring managers should feel comfortable knowing that you can work with the team and get the job done. The STAR approach can help you make the right impression in your resume.

TOPICS COVERED:
- Situation - Set the scene
- Task - Describe your role
- Action - Explain what you did
- Result - Demonstrate the impact

Let's talk about the STAR approach (STAR). This breaks down into four simple things: Situation, Task, Action, and Result. In the last chapter, we covered how to structure your resume and what to include in your resume. Now, we'll cover how to write those accomplishments in a way that really sells your qualifications. The STAR approach is within your grasp – just reach out and grab it! Too much on the nose with that analogy? Not to worry – you'll love the results even if the comedic attempts fall a bit short sometimes!

Here's why this approach is important: it will help you write your resume in a way that is informative, engaging, and also demonstrates that you really do have the qualifications and the competencies to do the work that is necessary for the position. This really comes into the idea of impact. It's a great thing to show that you have the capabilities to impact an organization positively. Hiring managers want to know they're making the right decision bringing you in for an interview or hiring you. There is such a thing as buyer's remorse when making hiring decisions. Once they sign on the job offer's dotted line – they're stuck with you. They need to feel like they are making the right choice because oftentimes they'll be working with this person for years to come. Why not help them make sure they choose the right person… you!

SITUATION - SET THE SCENE

Let's go ahead and get into exactly what this STAR approach is all about. First off: Situation. As you are describing your experiences, make sure you describe what the situation was. You don't need to go into a lot of detail, but at least provide some background information about why this was a big deal. This is a good time to set some context. Why was it that this was an important time of the year? Why was there a large dollar amount associated with the project? How was this a pivotal issue for the organization or for the agency? How would this action or activity change how the agency or the organization serves the public? Big picture, big scope stuff.

••• **CONNECT THE DOTS** •••

Let's give this strategy some attention! Identify a key accomplishment you want to convey in your resume. Next, write down the situation here. It helps to describe why this was needed or what the pain was that needed to be addressed.

_____

_____

_____

_____

_____

_____

_____

_____

_____

_____

_____

_____

_____

_____

_____

_____

_____

TASK - DESCRIBE YOUR ROLE

Next, think about the Task. What was it that you specifically needed to do? We know that there was this big context, there was this issue happening: there was the situation. The task is what you did to help address whatever that situation was. Think of a big action movie. The world is in peril and danger is all around. To make the difference and save the town, one lone hero steps into the fray to perform a specific action. Remember, your resume is all about you. Ask yourself, "What was the singular activity you did to address the mounting troubles?" This is your chance to be the hero in your resume. It's all about you, after all. ☺

Was this a plan or an activity that you needed to implement? Was it research? Was it the execution of a strategy? Did you need to conduct some analysis? Perhaps, do some research, speak with some people, and build coalitions? What were the actions or the activities that you needed to do? In short, what was your quest?

In this area, also make sure you are trying to help provide a little bit more information about what was happening. Did you need to speak with key individuals or were there key actions or activities that needed to occur? The more that the reader can place themselves into that situation and understand that you know what needs to happen, the better off you will be. The reader, the hiring manager, the selecting official - they should be able to think to themselves, "This individual has the experience that I need a person to have." You will be much more qualified in their eyes if you can demonstrate that you can do the work that they need someone to do. I mean, that's kind of why they're looking for people to hire in the first place, right? They are asking themselves, "Who has the experience that is needed to do the work that I have available right now?" Pretty straight forward.

••• CONNECT THE DOTS •••

When crafting the task, consider who assigned the work to you. A factor evaluation that human resources professionals often consider is the organizational setting or the position you're accountable to. The higher the setting (ex. reporting to an SES level or general officer military rank), the better your factor level rating will be.

_____

_____

_____

_____

_____

_____

_____

_____

_____

_____

_____

_____

_____

_____

_____

ACTION - EXPLAIN WHAT YOU DID

Next is the Action. What are the steps that you took to implement whatever the task was? If you needed, for example, to conduct some research, what actions did you take to conduct that research? Did you look at financial systems? Did you go over operation reports? Did you export data? Did you collaborate with others in order to get more content or more information available for people to use? If it was something more about project planning or project activities, what were the actions, or the steps that you took, to make sure that the task was completed? It should be clear enough to show that the action was in direct connection to the task you were given to address the needs of the situation. Think of a video game or a board game. What are the specific actions needed to complete the objective of the game? Move the knight five spaces to capture the queen, execute a forward pass to make the touchdown, buy up all of the properties to create a monopoly. These are the actions you took in order to meet the objective of the situation.

These actions should be able to demonstrate that you have the experiences and the competencies to really have the success that they're looking for in the job. Think of it this way: when you go to the store and you are looking at a couple of different products to purchase, you look at the back of each of them, you know, the little packaging and all that, and you read the specifications. This one has 38 megapixels. This one records in 4K. That's how we're able to make comparisons. The same thing happens with the hiring official. When they are comparing the different resumes or when they are conducting the interviews, they will say, "Well, this one person has this type of experience. While this other person took all of these actions that really helped their organization… and it just so happens that those are the actions that we are looking for as well – Let's bring this person in for an interview!" Hiring managers want to measure the qualifications of the people they are seeing against the needs of the opportunity. It makes sense when you stop to think about it. Wouldn't you want to choose a candidate that meets the qualifications you are looking for as well? Supervisors are looking to determine whether or not you are a good fit for the activity that they need. Remember, they want to feel comfortable about making their decision here. Hiring is one of the most critical aspects of their job description and it could be a bit tense for them. Especially in government, again, they may be working with this person for years to come. On top of that, many begin by looking at faceless names on a piece of paper. Help them help you by crafting a resume that speaks to their needs.

••• **CONNECT THE DOTS** •••

Now for the action portion. Capture what actions you took to directly address the challenge. Consider if you took any steps that were not done before or if your approach was not something others had considered trying. The more innovation you can convey in your example the better.

_____

_____

_____

_____

_____

_____

_____

_____

_____

_____

_____

_____

_____

_____

_____

RESULT - DEMONSTRATE THE IMPACT

So far, we have talked about Situation, Task, and Action. Now, here is the most important one of all of these: the Result. You want to show impact for the organization. Did you improve something? Did you decrease risk or issues or concerns? Did you have a large output? Was there a large dollar amount that was involved? Did this get turned around within a certain period of time? Did the organization accomplish its mission or objectives as a result of the actions that you had taken? These are the types of ideas that you can place into context to show that you are making a true impact and you are demonstrating results. Often as we are working with clients, we will see resumes that really describe only the actions of the activity. Almost like they just took the job description, copied it, pasted it into the resume and said, "Yep, that's what I did. Do you want to hire me?"

It's great that you're doing the work, but how does the hiring manager know that you can do the work well, or even at all? Just because it says on your resume that you did the work, does it demonstrate that you did the work well enough to do it for the organization you're hoping to join? Were you recognized for the work? Was there a positive impact on the organization? If you take a step back and think about it for a second, these are the sorts of things that really make your resume stand out. It's not enough to simply say, "Yeah, well, you know, I have done this for like 5 years, so I know what I'm doing." You need to show them just how good you are at the work and how those experiences have allowed you to be prepared for the next level. This is a big concept we need to make sure we cover.

We love helping you guys and want the best for you and the people we serve as public servants. So, here comes some honesty: Just because you've done the work for a long time doesn't mean you're qualified for the next level, or even deserve the next level. You have to demonstrate that you did this current level so well that you have developed the competencies needed to excel in the next level. Otherwise, for example, you'll be that manager or team lead that knows the work but can't manage a project or lead a team to save their life. Odds are, you've worked for a person like this before. Most, if not all, of us have. Worse yet, the managers often don't know they are part of the problem. Instead, many managers shift the blame back onto their teams. It's a cautionary tale – demonstrate and be ready for that next job. Your resume and reflection while writing it are a key aspect of not only getting the job, but excelling in the role as well. That's why this part of the resume writing process is so fundamental. Reflection is an incredible tool not just for writing a good summary of your qualifications, but also as a means to help you stand ready for your career growth.

Having said all that, make sure that the results you are crafting demonstrate a type of interest and a concern that a person could have when reviewing your application. They should look at it and think, "Wow, you know, this is really good. This is a person that can do some great stuff. Let me make sure that this moves on to the next level of review."

Having all of the components from this chapter put together is just a fantastic way to demonstrate that you have the qualifications necessary. And also, as a quick sidebar, by using the STAR approach, you have fantastic examples already developed and ready to go for your interview. When you're sitting there – on the brink of that dream job – if they say, *"Tell me about yourself,"* you'll be ready. We're telling you - you will have lots of great accomplishments to talk about! Plus, you've done the reflections and soul searching to be ready for that experience. There will be very little you won't be ready for in that conversation. In fact, you may find yourself shifting from thinking about your fit for them to their fit for you. There's nothing like knowing who you are, what you want out of a work experience, and what you're

THE GOV GEEKS | JAVIER AND KAREN LOPEZ

willing to say no to. Whoa… I just got goosebumps with that one!

In this chapter, we talked about the STAR approach: Situation, Task, Action, Result. Make sure that when you are writing your resume, you use this approach to really demonstrate your qualifications. You've done all of the work; you've had the impacts and the successes. So, make sure you are capturing it in your resume. Give yourself as much credit as possible. Be the hero in your resume that the hiring manager needs!

••• CONNECT THE DOTS •••

Now for the results. Capture what the value the organization experienced thanks to your work. Do your best to quantify this by showing an increased or decreased percentage, cost saving, and the like.

_____

_____

_____

_____

_____

_____

_____

_____

_____

_____

_____

_____

_____

_____

_____

_____

NOTES AND REFLECTIONS

Let's practice writing a few more accomplishments using the STAR approach. Remember the Situation, Task, Action, and Result.

Accomplishment 1

_____

_____

_____

_____

_____

_____

_____

Accomplishment 2

_____

_____

_____

_____

_____

_____

_____

Accomplishment 3

_____

_____

_____

_____

_____

_____

_____

INSIDER'S TIP

Developing your accomplishment write ups can present a unique choice of word challenge. Getting the right words on paper is a talent and one not easily developed. We should know, we went through a few drafts of this book and could still make a few improvements! But we found a tremendous asset in our careers you may be of interest in learning more about. From resume reviews and interview prep to performance assessments and budget justifications, accessible yet effective words and phrases are worth their weight in gold.

Enter Paul Falcone and his book 2600 *Phrases for Effective Performance Reviews*. Broken out by career field themes and activities, the book has ready to use descriptions to help you cut down on the resume writing heavy lifting. Simply review the table of contents for your subject area then effortlessly flip to the section of the book and boom! You've got tremendous phrases to use that concisely convey the words that have been eluding you.

Falcone, P. (2005). *2600 phrases for effective performance reviews: Ready-to-use words and phrases that really get results.* AMACOM.

CHAPTER 4:

FOCUS ON THE IMPACT

We want your resume to really stand out as the key individual that has qualified for the position. Hiring officials should look at your resume and think to themselves, "This is the type of person that we need in our organization - this is the person that will help us do what we need to do." Well, to get that done, you should be focused on impact in your resume. It's just like if you are writing a term paper, for instance. One of the bigger sets of questions that you can ask yourself as you are writing is to say, "So what? Why is this a good thing? Why should I be interested?" It's not enough to simply state what you did in your job. There's no way for anyone to interpret what level of quality you are offering just by listing what your role was. Give the reader something more to hold on to and visualize. They need to be enticed enough to want to read more and even meet you in person to see the real deal for themselves. Following the theme from our earlier chapters, wouldn't you want that type of person as an option if you were the hiring official? Of course, you would! So let's talk about impact.

TOPICS COVERED:
- Think about the hiring manager
- Answer the question, "So what?"
- Keep it relevant to the agency and mission
- Use the hiring official's perspective as a guiding light

THINK ABOUT THE HIRING MANAGER

When you are writing and you say, "Here are my tasks, here are my activities," be sure to ask: "Why is that a good thing?" and, "How did that impact the organization?" Keep the hiring manager in mind. Managers need to justify their selection to their supervisors (everyone has a boss in government) and to stakeholders. Your resume should reflect what a hiring manager should be reading and allow them to know that you are a qualified candidate. To be clear, job duties are not qualifications. The impact you've made while completing said duties are. Writing about the impact you've made shows how you've taken those duties and successfully realized accomplishments.

Hiring managers love to be able to connect how what you've done in the past can be repeated in their organization. This gives them comfort that you can do the job because you've done it already. They don't need to walk you through every little thing. They need help doing the work – that's why they're hiring for the job. They're not looking for someone that will give themselves more work in order to train and develop them. They want to scope out the work, set visions and expectations, and then delegate to you while monitoring issues. Impact is a very important thing!

Up next, we'll discuss three things for us to concentrate on when talking about focusing on your impact. The first one, again, is answering the simple question, "So what?" Second, really make sure that there is an agency and a mission relevance. Lastly, number three, use the hiring official's perspective as a guiding light.

••• CONNECT THE DOTS •••

Look at a job announcement that you're interested in applying for. Consider why the hiring manager needs this role filled. Is it a technical role that requires a level of expertise you have or a supervisory role where your leadership skills can shine? Write down a few skills you will emphasize in your resume to meet their needs.

_____

_____

_____

_____

_____

_____

_____

_____

_____

_____

_____

_____

_____

_____

_____

ANSWER THE QUESTION, "SO WHAT?"

One of the main things that you want to avoid when a person is evaluating your resume is for them to say, "Uhm... so what? I have people on my team that already do that." What is it about your experience that will help you demonstrate that you can do the work?

It's not just talking about activities or actions. Moving through the process, through the motions of the work, is not enough. For instance, your resume should not just list how you make a sandwich (delicious by the way). Instead, consider the impact that you making the sandwich had on others and use numbers to describe it. Try something like this: "Led a staff of X people to create Y-custom designed sandwiches that met the needs of Z attendees as a key health and wellness component of the agency's annual summit on nutrition." It demonstrates leadership, project management, scope of work, and impact on an agency objective. There's a reason why you do all of your work assignments. Connect with the bigger picture of why you do what you do, and write to it.

Managers have to guess or create leaps of logic to assume a person can do the work. Demonstrate that you know what the work is and that you can do it. As applicants, it's our responsibility to make sure we are answering that bigger question for them. At the end of the day, when they are looking at your resume, they will think, "Okay, yeah, I am excited about this person! I can't wait to bring them in for an interview and hear more about how they were able to do all of these great things." Then they can also start to play in their mind how your accomplishments and skills could actually help them do the work that they are needing to do. Your impact writing should allow them to readily see the fit in the organization, not guessing if you have the qualifications necessary. But we'll talk more about that in a little bit.

••• CONNECT THE DOTS •••

Consider how you will demonstrate that you know the work. Are there key terms or technical concepts that you are aware of or do you know of certain awards or accomplishments that they will take to mean you know about their work. Write down a few items you feel they should know you know.

_____

_____

_____

_____

_____

_____

_____

_____

_____

_____

_____

_____

_____

_____

_____

_____

_____

_____

_____

KEEP IT RELEVANT TO THE AGENCY AND MISSION

The whole idea behind public service is to really fulfill a mission or a purpose. The American people allow us as public servants to work in positions that serve the greater good. That's the job. Our ultimate boss is the public. We exist to serve the needs of others. That's the beauty and privilege of our work.

When you focus your resume on how you are impacting the agency itself or the organization's mission, it allows the hiring manager to understand that you have the frame of reference that allows the organization to move forward. It's not just about you, it's not about you saying, "Yeah, you know, I show up 9 to 5. I do this job and I go home and that's it." Well, I mean, we all work, we all have to have jobs in order to have mortgages and go to comic book conventions (or is that just us?). But at the end of the day, it's about something bigger. It's about serving a purpose, serving the well-being of others. In fact, you can trace the roots of the work of agencies directly to the Declaration of Independence or the Constitution. Let's not lose sight of that. We're here to do important work. Keeping an eye on that in your resume really helps it stand out, and it helps your work resonate with why you chose public service in the first place.

If you can voice that perspective as you are writing, you will show how you helped move an agency or an organization forward. How you helped accomplish a mission, how you helped manage a project, a program, or an activity in such a way that an individual was able to benefit. To give you some more ideas when you're writing, consider if you were able to save the agency money, improve efficiencies, improve operations, or expand operational capacity. Those are some of the many things that your hiring manager will look at and think, "This person gets it." They don't want to hire a person and then try to convince them to do a great job when they are there. If you are demonstrating that you know how and why it's important to do great things, then they can project into your experiences and know you are the type of person that will be able to do the work because you care about the mission.

This is an interesting point, really. Agencies spend so much time and money on employee engagement, professional development activities like training and team building, and performance management. For them, they'd like to see a candidate that finds passion in their work and won't need an abundance of additional poking and prodding to get them to perform. Show them that you get why you do your job and connect with the mission. In the end, this approach is of course good for you as you'll be a top contender for the role, but it's also good for them and the public. As a taxpayer, don't you want to have your dollars paying people who want to offer you the value you deserve as a citizen? You want people who do the work they're paid to do because you deserve the results of it as a member of society. Not to get too "founding father" sounding in all of this but really, we're talking about public service here. This is what our work is all about!

••• CONNECT THE DOTS •••

Think of the agency as a machine that needs components to operate. What items do you have that will help it run smoothly or avoid issues? The more you can demonstrate a partnership mindset, the better.

_____

_____

_____

_____

_____

_____

_____

_____

_____

_____

_____

_____

_____

_____

_____

_____

_____

_____

USE THE HIRING OFFICIAL'S PERSPECTIVE AS A GUIDING LIGHT

While we've mentioned this theme throughout this chapter, it's important to take a second and to think through your resume from their eyes (empathy is a big thing in this book, by the way. It's all about relationship building!). If you were the hiring official, part of the selection panel, or a partner stakeholder who will work with this person day in and day out, what are the things that you would care about? Take a look at the job description and see where it lists activities, responsibilities, job duties, requirements, qualifications, all of that sort of stuff. Then think to yourself, "Okay, why are they asking for that?" For example, why would a person need to have access to certain financial systems, programs, or activities? Why would they need particular skills like monitoring, analysis, or management? Well, if those are what they are looking for, then you can understand that perhaps they would like to have a person to use them to execute the job well. Essentially, they're giving you what they want you to be able to do right up front. They're setting the expectation that the qualified candidate will have those experiences and qualifications.

If you were to write your resume explaining that not only do you have those competencies, those qualifications, and those skills, but you have a great track record of implementing them in a way that brings about a lot of success... you're golden! I mean, that's the thing that they should look at and think, "Yes! I can see where this person is coming from – that totally makes sense. They have the right type of systems access, they have the right experience, and they understand the bigger picture. They are qualified to do this work." That's what we're aiming for here. To place your qualifications in the mind of the decision makers as the key person to do the work.

Whatever point you are at in your career, if it's entry or mid-level, if it's senior or executive, we are all part of a bigger plan or objective for how the agency or the organization goes about accomplishing what it needs to accomplish. If you can describe that you have a good understanding of the impact that your role has for the whole operation – that's fantastic. You could say my work is to do this, but it's better to say that your work connects to a bigger objective. This demonstrates your influence or impact on bigger things – which then serves the public. Show them you're proud of your work. That you get the bigger idea of what your work is. Show them how your work has moved organizations forward.

We love this fantastic example. This is a legendary tale, or inspirational reflection if you will, where John F. Kennedy was visiting a NASA facility. He ran into one of the people on the janitorial staff and said, "Hi, I am John Kennedy. What do you do here?" And the person answered, "Well, Mr. President, I helped put a man on the moon" (Both-Nwabuwe et al., 2017). That's the bigger picture. It's not just the person saying, you know, I do this task and I go home. No, it's about this collectiveness, this teamwork – we are all in this together. The more that you can show that perspective to the hiring official, the more excited they will be about the work that you could do there. That's the type of person that they want on the team. Someone that sees the bigger picture and the connections to why that organization or team really gets stuff done.

In this chapter, we've talked about focusing on impact for your resume. We looked at three things: Answering the bigger question: "So what?", making sure that you are adding relevance to the agency and the mission, and lastly, looking at the perspective of the hiring official.

When you do all of this as you are writing your resume, you will start to see that there really is a big impact that you will have because you are directly connected to what they care about. You are making an impact. This is why we're here. Thank you for your service!

••• CONNECT THE DOTS •••

When capturing your past experiences, keep in mind that your organization needed your work to make something happen. Use this perspective to craft your resume. How did your work help the team reach a certain goal? Help them see that you are a significant factor in the success of the effort.

_____

_____

_____

_____

_____

_____

_____

_____

_____

_____

_____

_____

_____

_____

_____

_____

NOTES AND REFLECTIONS

Take a look at the target skills you captured in Chapter 2. What is it about your experience that will help you demonstrate that you can do this work?

_____

_____

_____

_____

_____

_____

_____

How has that work impacted the mission of your organization?

_____

_____

_____

_____

_____

_____

_____

What about this would be appealing to the hiring manager?

_____

_____

_____

_____

_____

_____

_____

INSIDER'S TIP

Staying relevant to the agency mission in your examples is a solid strategy to help demonstrate capabilities relevant to the needs of the hiring manager. Sticking to the themes of the job duties can help but knowing why they're important in the first place is just as important. Selecting officials want to know that you can see the bigger picture behind the activities. More than being able to accomplish a simple task, they want to see if you know how your work impacts the organization. After all, would you want to select a person that is disengaged and tough to motivate to do the work or an involved and supportive colleague who feels a connection to their work? It's easy when you say it that way, right?

Peter H. Daly and Michael Watkins, with Cate Reavis, put together a tremendous book called *The First 90 Days in Government* to help us learn how to do just that, especially chapter 7: Achieve Alignment. Pick up a copy of this book to help you develop a strong resume and make the most of your career in government.

Daly, P. H., Watkins, M., & Reavis, C. (2006). *The first 90 days in government: Critical success strategies for new public managers at all levels* (1st ed.). Harvard Business Review Press.

CHAPTER 5:

MAKE IT RELEVANT

We have seen many resume approaches attempt to be all things to all of the positions they're interested in. While it's good to express a diverse array of talents and expertise, the approach falls short if it is not pertinent to the needs of the position. Aligning your resume with the job series, the target job itself, and (most importantly) what's important to you , is a fundamental part of a solid resume.

Writing a solid resume is all about including what is compelling for decision makers. In this chapter, we'll talk about how you can "Make It Relevant" so you can make it rain with that new salary!

The experiences you write about need to have a strong degree of relevance, not just obviously from what you've done and where you've been, but relevant to the individual that is making the ultimate decision: the selecting official. If you make your resume relevant for them, odds are you will be a top consideration. We've talked a bit about writing strategies in larger terms. Now we'll dive into some real specifics like where to find the content, buzz words, and the like. We can break this down into three simple items. First: make it relevant to your job series. Second: your target job. Lastly (and most importantly), what is important to you. Let's begin!

TOPICS COVERED:
- Make it relevant to your job series
- Make it relevant to your target job
- Make it relevant to what is important to you
- Make it relevant to your job series

When working in the federal government you learn that everyone has a job series. It could be for instance, a 0343, Management and Program Analyst. Those four numbers describe the type of work you'll be doing, what experiences are needed for the job, and how agencies determine who is qualified for the position. Why is all of this important? I'm so glad you asked!

The US Office of Personnel Management (OPM) breaks out all government positions into job series numbers. Those numbers then relate to specific job qualifications that are necessary for that position. This allows the government to say that a person working in a certain department that is in a certain job series at a certain grade level will be able to do the same type of work as someone else in the same department, job series and grade level at another agency or organization. It's a way of setting a baseline standard across the many government positions. It also creates a uniform way to define responsibilities and work expectations in order to have some equity across the board. Otherwise, one agency would pay less for the same services or demand more of individuals than in others. Is the system foolproof? Of course not. But it does help by setting a standard to begin conversations that would otherwise not be possible.

Now, it's very, very true that some positions are a little bit different than others. There are some unique factors for each of the different areas based on mission requirements and the like. Still, with that said, there's at least a baseline. This is important when you're writing your resume, because you are writing towards those qualifications that are needed for that individual job. Writing to the baseline will help you demonstrate that you meet the baseline requirements... and more. Make sure you're looking at OPM's requirements, make sure you're looking at the descriptions that are necessary for that one position, and allow yourself room to really make it relevant. As you can imagine, there's a lot to cover here. To do this topic justice and give you the most value, we'll cover more of OPM requirements in the next chapter.

••• **CONNECT THE DOTS** •••

Later in the book we'll begin looking at OPM's job series numbers more closely. For now, conduct some career
market research on USAJOBS.gov for positions you're
interested in applying for. Along with the job titles, write
down the three job series numbers below. You'll find
them under the 'overview' section on the right of the
page listed as "Job family (Series)."

_____

_____

_____

_____

_____

_____

_____

_____

_____

_____

_____

_____

_____

_____

_____

MAKE IT RELEVANT TO YOUR TARGET JOB

Now, the other great thing about making your resume relevant is that you are designing your resume to meet the needs of the specific position that you're applying to. You need to look back at all of the positions you've had up until now and answer the bigger question: "how is what you've done before relevant to what you're applying to do now?" This really is an interesting question. We have worked with more than a few clients that have done a lot of different things in their career. That's awesome. It's great to get a plethora of experiences to identify what you have a strong passion for and reasonable expectations for career growth. At one point or another, they think to themselves, "Well, gosh, I don't think anything that I've done before is relevant to what I'm applying for now." A common misconception. The key is to focus on what is required in the job and what is transferable from across your career.

If you take the time to reflect back on your work, you may realize you have more in common with the work requirements than you once thought. Find the key performance words in the job description. They're usually verbs like plans, evaluates, leads, promotes, analyzes, reviews, writes, conducts, etc. Then consider when you have done that in the past. Maybe you led a team of volunteers for a church function, or managed a project or activity in an office job. There are tons of areas to consider here, if you take the time to consider them. Now, compare what you've done to what the job series requires. From there, you can add up the years of experience you've earned planning, evaluating, executing, leading, etc. You may have tons of great experience you're not giving yourself credit for. The experiences demonstrate that you have the qualifications necessary for this particular position! Looking back with that lens of what your job series requires allows you to really describe the work that you've done in a way that allows the hiring official to understand that you have the experience necessary. Plus, in interviews, you can say that you've been doing that type of work for years and understand the activities from a myriad of levels. It means a lot to hiring managers that you know how to execute the work at an entry level and lead the work at an experienced level. If you've got the experience, work it, work it, own it! A little too much Pretty Woman? Maybe so. We love that movie. 😄

Now, secondly, focus on your target job. That one job that you're hitting submit for or applying to is not necessarily the only time you can use that resume. Not at all. The thing about making it relevant is that you're writing to that entire job series and the requirements of that type of job. Other careers in the same job series are looking for the same kind of work expertise. By building your resume against the qualifications of one position, you're demonstrating the qualifications necessary for other ones as well. A lot of times, as we're working with clients, they might say, "So you're telling me I have to write a brand-new resume for every single position that I'm applying to?! I'm applying to hundreds of jobs. This is totally unrealistic. I can't write that many resumes!" Well, no worries. You don't have to. You're building your resume for that job series and all the opportunities within that area.

Earlier, when we mentioned that there can be two jobs in the same series but in different departments, we meant it's still the same type of work that is done in both positions. From one agency to another, the work is reasonably similar, so they have the same job series. For instance, a Management Analyst (Management and Program Analysis job series 0343) at the US Department of State should be able to do the same work at the US Department of Agriculture if it is the same career level. Yes, there will be some differences. Obviously this is true. But there is still enough similarity for the shared job series. Otherwise, they wouldn't have classified that job under that series in the first place. Makes sense, right? If you are writing towards what is common, amongst all of these different positions in the same series, you are writing towards each of those areas that you can apply to. So, target your job series and write to your heart's content!

Let's go into more detail about what exactly that means using an example. Consider what requirements come with working as a Management Analyst. Consider the list of sample requirements below, then think through what past experiences you've had that will demonstrate that you have the qualifications to do the work directly in that specific job.

1. Knowledge and skill to gather, assemble, and analyze facts, draw conclusions, devise solutions to problems, and identify changes and trends.

2. Skill in applying analytical and evaluative techniques to the identification, consideration, and resolution of issues or problems of a procedural or factual nature.

3. Ability to communicate effectively, both orally and in writing, to gain cooperation from others through tact, courtesy, and diplomacy.

4. Skill in conducting interviews with supervisors and employees to obtain information about organizational missions, functions, and work procedures.

5. Ability to access or locate information through the use of a personal computer and software programs.

Tailor your resume to the job series that you're applying for to allow yourself the opportunity to show that you have the experiences necessary for those jobs. It's not necessarily just the job series, but also specifically the target job itself. You should be able to sit down in an interview, and when they say, "Tell us about why you feel you're qualified for this position," you can relate all of the experiences that you've had that connect with that job. It allows you to demonstrate that you are really qualified for the position.

••• **CONNECT THE DOTS** •••

While researching your positions for the job series numbers, take a look at the "duties" section of the job announcements. Note any term or skill patterns you see across your target jobs in the space below. Those are the items to focus on when making your resume relevant to your target job.

_____

_____

_____

_____

_____

_____

_____

_____

_____

_____

_____

_____

_____

_____

_____

_____

_____

MAKE IT RELEVANT TO WHAT IS IMPORTANT TO YOU

Next, and again, most importantly is to ask a simple question. What is important to you? This is a tricky one because it goes beyond the obvious. We all want good pay, a nice work environment, and nice benefits. But why that specific job? Why that career field? There are lots of ways to make money and lots of jobs in government. For you, what is important about that specific role that makes you want to apply for it? Why would having that job be something you really wanted? Something more than getting away from a challenging boss or a toxic work environment. You should know what is important for you. Otherwise, you'll just find more problems in this job as well. We want you to be happy and fulfilled in your work, and can sensibly assume you want the same thing. So, build this requirement into the job search up front!

As you're reflecting back on your different positions (full time, part time, volunteer, project based, etc.), think to yourself, "What are the things that I did that really brought me joy? What are the things that I really cared about?" When you find the things that you were passionate about, you'll begin to compile a list of the tasks or activities that really engaged you. Write to these items in your resume. Odds are when a person is evaluating your resume, they'll see what these passions are. If they connect with them as well, you'll be happy doing that work. Both of you will find commonality right from the beginning and build the foundation of a great professional relationship. At the end of the day, you want to be in a job that you care about. It should be that Friday afternoon feeling versus the Sunday evening feeling. Here's how that works.

Friday afternoon, the weekend is coming up, everyone is like, "Woo hoo! I finally get to do all this stuff that I want to do." That's what the feeling should be when you're describing your experiences in the resume. You care about these things, you're passionate about these things, or these are some of the things that you actually look forward to doing. That's a great way of describing these experiences. When a person that is doing the hiring can match their interest with your interest, you find a lot more fulfillment. Compare that to the Sunday afternoon feeling. We're pretty sure you know what we are talking about. You're sitting there thinking, "Yeah, life is great, Sunday is wonderful." Then, that little thought comes into your mind… "Oh no! Tomorrow is Monday. I have to go to work tomorrow! I have to go do this or I have to go do that." Not a great feeling. There's a lot of negative energy around that one. If you focus on what is positive from your experiences and what you care about in your resume, you stand a much better chance of doing that work consistently. When you're doing those kinds of activities day in and day out, your job will be fun because it's not really work - it's stuff that you enjoy. That is making it relevant to you. This is what is important to you. So why not go for it?

In this chapter, we talked about three different things that can help you make your resume relevant. First off, focus on the job series that you are applying to. Second, focus on your target job. The job that you're really looking for, the one that is meaningful for you. Third, focus on what's important for you. The more you tell people what you want and what you like, the easier it is for them to see what you want to do. Plus, if you're applying to a place that doesn't have any of the things that you like or the things that you want to do, why would you want to work there anyways? Find the thing that makes you happy and brings you joy and fulfillment, and then go for that. If there's a job out there that relates to your passion... awesome, go for it!

••• CONNECT THE DOTS •••

This is where it gets really meaningful! Take a moment to list the items you're genuinely excited about in your job search. What work do you want to do? What experiences have you enjoyed in the past? Design your resume around these as well to build the potential of you working on them in the future.

_____

_____

_____

_____

_____

_____

_____

_____

_____

_____

_____

_____

_____

_____

_____

_____

_____

NOTES AND REFLECTIONS

Consider the target skills you captured earlier. How will these help you in your career search?

_____

_____

_____

_____

_____

_____

_____

What about your experiences applies to your target job series? What could you add to appeal to Human Capital reviewers?

_____

_____

_____

_____

_____

_____

_____

Consider the work you are looking to do. How is what you've done before relevant to that work?

_____

_____

_____

_____

_____

_____

_____

Here's a truly important question – What about these experiences is relevant to what you want to do (not just what you've *already done*)?

_____

_____

_____

_____

_____

_____

_____

INSIDER'S TIP

We've seen a true aspect of joy come to life in people who pursue work that is meaningful for them. Able to put things in perspective and enjoy some of the most mundane aspects of their jobs, these people are shining examples of how we can each lead an energetic and impactful career. Think of someone you've worked with or seen who enjoys their profession. What characteristics would you use to describe them? A healthy smile or enthusiasm, perhaps? What about a pattern of getting lost in their work or taking joy in the processes? All are good indicators of a person aligned with their work. But how to create that for ourselves, you ask? Enter our friend and fellow coach John Neral.

John's book *Show up: Six strategies to lead a more energetic and impactful career* gives us a methodology to build strong relationships and do the work that is most important to us. We've seen his approach change lives and hope it is of value to you as well!

Neral, J. (2020). *Show up: Six strategies to lead a more energetic and impactful career.* John Neral Coaching.

CHAPTER 6:

KNOW WHAT OPM SAYS YOU NEED

O PM - the US Office of Personnel Management – is a big deal in the federal government. As the chief Human Resources component and personnel policy management component (US Office of Personnel Management [OPM]), this organization is responsible for a host of responsibilities. From writing job series descriptions to making sure that the policies and procedures are in place, they are the backbone to ensuring selecting officials can hire really good people to work for the American people. So, why is it important to make sure that you know what OPM says you need to have? Well, they essentially set the rule book for the process and give you the roadmap to get into government. If you want to get in or land a promotion, you should develop a strategy that meets the requirements they have laid out. In other words, know the rules you're being evaluated against.

In an earlier chapter, we mentioned that this topic needed a space all to itself. It is definitely an important one,but not necessarily complicated. Once you get a few of these concepts down in your writing, you'll be in a much better position to excel in your job search. Heck, these are great tips that you'll use time and again throughout your career! In this chapter, we'll talk about three things to help you write a fantastic resume so you can pass the OPM test. To begin, look at OPM's Handbook of Occupational Groups and Families. Second, know the position's hiring factors. Lastly, compare your competencies. When you add all three, you'll have a better sense of where your resume stands.

TOPICS COVERED:
- Use OPM's Handbook of Occupational Groups and Families
- Know the position's hiring factors
- Compare your competencies

Use OPM's Handbook of Occupational Groups and Families

Let's talk a little bit more about the first one. The Handbook of Occupational Groups and Families is a goldmine of information for really everyone that is applying for a federal job. The resource provides general information used in determining the occupational series, title, grade, and pay system for positions performing white collar work in the Federal Government (US Office of Personnel Management [OPM]). It's completely online and it's entirely free. It was written to help agencies begin classifying their positions. Managers need to know what level they have a mission need for so they'll know how much the position will cost their agency. It also helps them define the scope of responsibilities reasonable for the position. They can't expect to get the work of an entire Division, Unit, or Branch from one person and pay them an entry-level salary. Thank goodness it doesn't work that way!

Here's a quick note on the handbook. At over 200 pages, this is a hefty document with a lot of nuances and helpful links. This book isn't the be-all and end-all of OPM's policies and procedures. Believe us, there are other books and training for that! Human Resource experts and career public servants can give you stories and policy descriptions to take up your afternoon. But you may not have the time for all of that right now. Instead, we'd like to give you the heads up on the document and, more importantly, help you understand how to use it to write an awesome resume. That's why you're here, right?

The handbook is broken up into two parts: White Collar Occupations and Trade, Craft, or Labor Occupations. As you may imagine, white collar jobs are typically office-based positions while the trade, craft, and labor jobs are those outside of an office environment. White collar jobs run the gamut from social sciences and veterinary medicine, to information technology and legal work. But the government needs much more work than that. There are tons of great jobs that can be found in agencies of all shapes and sizes. Looking at the trade, craft, and labor jobs you have positions from barbering and bartending, to welding and woodworking at your discretion.

Each of the positions are sorted into a job group or family. Groups correspond to White Collar Occupations, while Families correspond to Trade, Craft, and Labor Occupations. The Human Resources Management Group has positions like Equal Employment Opportunity Series while the Fabric and Leather Work Family has Upholstering. You can either head straight to the job you're looking for by doing a simple search in the document or scroll through the descriptions to find what is best for you. For instance, if your desired job involves management analysis, scroll on down to the 0300 series to see Office Services Group jobs (there are usually tons of positions in that area by the way). But that's not all! Once you've found your position, the handbook includes a description of the work and a link to documents like Job Grading Standards and Position Classification Flysheets. This is where we hit the really good stuff.

These documents describe important items like titles, nature of the work, position classification standards, and grade level descriptions. In other words, they're giving you the answers to the OPM test! This is what your applications are evaluated against. If you know what they're looking for, and use the information to show them how you meet their needs, you stand an incredible chance of being deemed qualified for the role and ultimately selected! Let that sink in for a bit. They're telling you what standards are needed to be qualified for the job. There's not a lot of guess work here. Just tell them how you meet the qualifications in a compelling manner and you're well on your way. You're welcome. Mic drop. #TheGovGeeksAreMyHeroes. Okay, maybe not that intense. We'll dial it back…

These documents go to great lengths to say what an individual should know or have expertise around in order to do that kind of work for the government. Then it even goes an extra step, and it says, here are some examples of how a person could show that they're qualified to do this work. They also show different concepts that a person should know and experience levels they should have to be qualified for the work. OPM even breaks all of these areas down into a rating criterion. This gives you a sense of what they're looking for in an applicant.

We've had a whole lot of clients, colleagues, and friends tell us about their challenges getting deemed qualified over the years. Many are truly well-credentialed and dedicated people who would make excellent members of the civil service. Unfortunately, their resumes simply did not convey those qualifications. Their whole lives —and by extension the lives of others as our work serves the public – could have changed with terrific government jobs if they had only written their resumes to these criteria. That's the big picture we're talking about here. Using the handbook gives you immense insight into what agencies are really looking for, and guides you in a way to help you convey your expertise to them. Really, if this was the only thing you took from this book, you'd be in a great position to make the job certification lists. We have spent a decent amount of time on this part, but we hope you have found it worthwhile!

••• **CONNECT THE DOTS** •••

Let's take a moment to look at the handbook itself. Hop online and navigate to OPM's webpage below. Here you'll find position classification standards and guides to learn how agencies define occupations, establish official position titles, and describe work activities. What strikes you most when you look at these materials?

https://www.opm.gov/policy-data-oversight/classification-qualifications/classifying-general-schedule-positions/

_____

_____

_____

_____

_____

_____

_____

_____

_____

_____

_____

_____

_____

_____

KNOW THE POSITION'S HIRING FACTORS

While you're looking at the handbook, check out the hiring factors. OPM invests a lot of time creating rating factors or criteria to help ensure applicants are evaluated fairly and against a set of standards. We do the same thing all the time, though we may not recognize it. For instance, say you're wondering where to go out to eat on Saturday night or you're deciding what movie to watch. As you're making these different decisions, you may say, for example, "You know, I am in the mood for pizza" or, "I'm craving a certain type of pasta" based on the criteria you're interested in to meet the needs of your night. One type of movie genre may make you laugh or feel good, while another might give you a bit of a rush from feeling a little scared or excited (we recommend something yummy and a comedy by the way). You have a desired outcome and are creating criteria or standards to weigh options against. Restaurants and movie production companies know what sorts of things you may find interesting and create products to meet your expectations. They're there for you when you go looking for those options. You could be the same for OPM and agencies. You know what they're looking for, so design your resume to meet their needs. To run this metaphor to the ground, you could be the perfect movie for them! On that note…

THE GOV GEEKS | JAVIER AND KAREN LOPEZ

we think we'd be an inspirational movie with a lot of superhero action scenes.

OPM has done the same thing (the standards not the action movie stuff). They're listing the hiring factors that a person should demonstrate to show that they are qualified for the position. If you're writing your resume towards what those evaluation factors are, you are well on your way to demonstrating that you have the qualifications that are necessary for the position. This handbook has the hiring factors - you just have to use them to your advantage.

••• **CONNECT THE DOTS** •••

Now that you have seen the handbook, navigate to your target job series options. Take a moment to review them to determine which one(s) you like the most. Write down your top numbers and titles here.

_____

_____

_____

_____

_____

_____

_____

_____

_____

_____

_____

_____

_____

_____

_____

_____

_____

_____

COMPARE YOUR COMPETENCIES

Next, the handbook also provides examples to explain how those factors can be demonstrated in a resume. Yup – they even give you models to help you see what they are talking about. Lots of nice people over in OPM. Using these you can evaluate whether you have similar examples. It's a terrific opportunity for you to consider your work history by looking back and reflecting on your experiences. Take a second to step back and think, "Okay, I really want this job. I am really excited about this type of work. Now, where is it that I've done this type of work before?" Think back to all of your positions. These could be both volunteer and paid positions. Consider the verbs they use as part of this. Words like manage, evaluate, review, lead, study, execute, etc. These are the words that you can connect your experiences with in order to show that you have the necessary experience for that work and that level of responsibility. From there, use those experiences to write your resume.

Lastly, compare your qualifications. Consider everything in the handbook that relates to your target position. Think of the objectives and hiring factors that OPM says an applicant needs for this position. Then, be honest with yourself. Has your resume done enough to give you as much credit as possible? Are your skills and qualifications presented in a compelling and applicable way? This is a wonderful moment for you to see just how qualified you are. To see how your work experience reflects the level you could perform in. Be proud of all that you have accomplished and know that you can do the work in this new job. There's nothing like having the proof right in front of you to help you see that you can do this!

When you look at these different items, you can consider the hiring factors for each grade level for yourself. If you know that you have the experiences for that grade level, then you should feel qualified enough to apply for those positions. You have the qualifications needed and have demonstrated them in your resume. Plus, you can compare your competencies for future jobs as well. You know what you have and don't have. You have all you need to build your roadmap to the next job, and even the job after that, right in front of you. When considering jobs or speaking with managers in interviews, you can judge for yourself just how much experience you can gain there and how it will help you continue to chart your career trajectory. In this way, you are in charge of your career. You're building the steps needed to reach even higher heights. It's all right there for you to use!

So often, when we're meeting with clients, we talk about these very issues. We hear real concerns people feel about their value or competency level. The root is in their un-awareness. How could they know if they were or were not qualified if they don't know the factors that indicate if they are or are not? It's like a blind guess! It's easy to leave it up to managers to tell us if we're qualified for the next level. That's where a lot of apprehension comes from when applying to jobs – not knowing if we are actually qualified for something. It's compounded further by our resumes. If your resume does not give you the credit you deserve or properly demonstrate your qualifications, you're doing yourself a disservice. Odds are, you're more qualified than you realize! Otherwise, you're apt to be passed over for promotions or continually apply for positions only to not get referred or brought in for interviews. It happens, but you don't have to let this happen to you.

This is it. This is the answer you've been waiting for... drum roll please... When you look at these factors, when you look at these competencies, you can see your qualifications for yourself. You can save yourself from feeling you need another degree, certification, or decade of work experience to finally feel like you have the qualifications necessary. This information is empowering. You're not putting the decision about your career happiness in someone else's hands or delaying what you have earned just because someone else feels you're not ready for it just yet.

Alright, there you go, that's it for this chapter. We covered three main things here. First, look at OPM's Handbook of Occupational Groups and Families. Second, consider OPM's hiring factors. Lastly, look a little bit more introspectively by comparing your competencies to determine your qualifications. These are the big things for you. Take the time to apply the lessons here and you'll see the results. It has worked for us and we hope you'll find the value in it as well.

••• **CONNECT THE DOTS** •••

As you look through the handbook, begin capturing how your resume aligns with the samples. Oftentimes, the growth point comes from finding tweaking opportunities after seeing the examples. Considering what you see, how can you update your resume?

_____

_____

_____

_____

_____

_____

_____

_____

_____

_____

_____

_____

_____

_____

_____

NOTES AND REFLECTIONS

List out your top target job series numbers. Which one appeals the most to you? Why?

_____

_____

_____

_____

_____

_____

Now, look for those jobs on USAJOBS. Which one has the most opportunities available?

_____

_____

_____

_____

_____

_____

As you narrow down your options, what are the hiring factors for each?

_____

_____

_____

_____

_____

_____

_____

What competencies do you have that match up for them?

_____

_____

_____

_____

_____

_____

_____

INSIDER'S TIP

What does your office look like these days? Many of our clients and colleagues have remarked that it is filled with the same sort of energy (good or bad) it had before the pandemic and that the staffing levels are tied directly to it. The office place of yesteryear is much different than we know it today. The federal government is not immune to the highs and lows of changing workplace cultures. In fact, it may be argued that it is even more so given the culture shock many experienced while working remotely. Where this leaves us is up to each individual and we know of a fantastic resource you could use.

The Office is Dead, Now What?: A Post-Pandemic Field Guide for Leadership walks readers down a path that covers workplace expectations, evolving workplace designs, and updated leadership behaviors. As you compare your competencies and write to your strengths, consider what the workplace needs now and in the future. Write about how you can make a difference for others and lead effectively.

Spatola, M. (2023). *The office is dead, now what?: A pos-pandemic field guide for leadership.* New Degree Press.

CHAPTER 7:

WRITE FOR THE FUTURE

The future is calling. It's right here – right now! I hope we're selling the drama of all this (nervous chuckle). Let's get to the point. You need to write your resume for the job series or career path you're applying for – not what you did previously and hope the hiring manager will see some areas of interest that are applicable to their needs. Solid resume writing is about targeting your goals. The challenge many people have (including ourselves before we learned this strategy) is spending time saying everything that was done but not making it relevant to the objective at hand. The key is to demonstrate the experiences that you've had and to connect them directly with the position that you are applying for here and now. The future is here and now - makes more sense now, right?

Let's go ahead and break this down into three easy and fun-filled steps. First, how does your experience demonstrate the capacity for future competency? Next, write to the hiring factors of the next grade level. In other words, describe how you have experience doing work related to the next level in your career. Third, show them you can play at the next level.

TOPICS COVERED:

- How does your experience demonstrate the capacity for future competency?
- Write to the hiring factors of the next grade level
- Show them you can play at the next level

HOW DOES YOUR EXPERIENCE DEMONSTRATE THE CAPACITY FOR FUTURE COMPETENCY?

You may ask,"How do you go about showing future competency if you haven't experienced it yet?" The thing is that you have already done them, but just haven't realized it yet. That's a key factor in your resume writing. You need to know the expectations of what you're getting yourself into and demonstrate you know what you're doing. A hiring manager wants to select someone that can take work off of their plate, not add more to it. A common thought selecting officials have when considering whom to hire is their ability to perform on the job and in their absence. For instance, they may think, "Can I send this person to a meeting with my peers or leadership and know that they can handle the work?" To feel comfortable with the hiring decision, they need to see your resume demonstrate specific experiences where you have performed at a level that they're hiring for. Few leaders spend their days thinking about how they can do the work of the entire branch or unit all by themselves. Remember, leaders develop leaders, while managers develop followers. Go for the environment that will help you rise to your highest potential, and then help you grow beyond that.

Take a second and think through what it is that you are applying to do. If you were to look at the job announcement, if you were to look at the duties and the descriptions about what the work is, you should be able to demonstrate that you have the skills necessary to do that job and then some. Say you are applying for a promotion or something that is the next step up or a higher level. How can a person determine if you have the qualifications necessary to do the job? You have to demonstrate what your competencies are. Lots of people have catchy words in the summary section of their resume like hard-working, self-starter, or experienced leader. While those are good, are you demonstrating that you have actually done that in your resume? If you were brought in for an interview, could you give examples of how your hard work and leadership impacted the agency without needing direct guidance from your boss? Put those experiences in your resume and let your qualifications shine. It's not enough to say you have the qualifications – you have to show them off!

In order to do this, one of the best things is to know exactly what is to be expected of you in the position. While looking at the job duties, review the mission of the organization and the role the position plays within it. From there, look backwards at all of your positions and ask yourself when you have done similar things. You may realize that you have a stronger track record of data analysis or project management than you realize. In fact, you should be able to count how many years of experience you actually have in a certain area. Then, you can total those years up and add them to your summary statement like this: "22 years of progressive leadership experience directing projects at the local, state, and federal levels." Pretty cool, right?

This way, when you are writing your resume, or when you are sitting in the interview, you can confidently say that you have X years of experience doing program analysis or whatever the subject area is. That is real quality, because you are not just saying, "Yeah, I did all of this other stuff, but I think I will try this new thing. Want to hire me?" Now, you are showing that you have the qualifications and the expertise necessary to do that type of work. Plus, this is a real confidence booster. When you total up all of the awesomeness that is you and place it in one spot, you get a sense of your value in that field. You can stand ready to speak to your expertise confidently and in an engaging manner. This helps you spend less time speaking to your experiences or explaining your work, and more time connecting your competencies to your target agency. That's what really stands out to selection officials. Give them every reason to say yes to you. The more enthusiastic they are, the better your chances of getting the position and setting your negotiation expectations as well.

••• **CONNECT THE DOTS** •••

Time to think about the future! What qualifications do you consider to be the best indicators of future performance?

_____

_____

_____

_____

_____

_____

_____

_____

_____

_____

_____

_____

_____

_____

_____

_____

_____

_____

_____

_____

WRITE TO THE HIRING FACTORS OF THE NEXT GRADE LEVEL

SALARY TABLE 2023-DCB
INCORPORATING THE 4.1% GENERAL SCHEDULE INCREASE AND A LOCALITY PAYMENT OF 32.49%
FOR THE LOCALITY PAY AREA OF WASHINGTON-BALTIMORE-ARLINGTON, DC-MD-VA-WV-PA
TOTAL INCREASE: 4.86%
EFFECTIVE JANUARY 2023

Annual Rates by Grade and Step

Grade	Step 1	Step 2	Step 3	Step 4	Step 5	Step 6	Step 7	Step 8	Step 9	Step 10
1	$ 27,822	$ 28,756	$ 29,679	$ 30,601	$ 31,525	$ 32,065	$ 32,981	$ 33,903	$ 33,940	$ 34,809
2	31,284	32,028	33,064	33,940	34,323	35,332	36,342	37,352	38,361	39,371
3	34,135	35,273	36,411	37,549	38,687	39,825	40,963	42,101	43,239	44,378
4	38,317	39,595	40,872	42,149	43,426	44,703	45,981	47,258	48,535	49,812
5	42,870	44,299	45,729	47,158	48,588	50,018	51,447	52,877	54,306	55,736
6	47,789	49,382	50,974	52,567	54,159	55,752	57,344	58,937	60,529	62,122
7	53,105	54,875	56,645	58,415	60,185	61,955	63,725	65,495	67,265	69,035
8	58,811	60,772	62,733	64,694	66,654	68,615	70,576	72,537	74,498	76,459
9	64,957	67,122	69,287	71,452	73,617	75,782	77,947	80,111	82,276	84,441
10	71,531	73,916	76,301	78,686	81,071	83,455	85,840	88,225	90,610	92,995
11	78,592	81,211	83,830	86,450	89,069	91,688	94,308	96,927	99,546	102,166
12	94,199	97,339	100,479	103,619	106,759	109,899	113,039	116,179	119,319	122,459
13	112,015	115,749	119,482	123,216	126,949	130,683	134,416	138,150	141,884	145,617
14	132,368	136,780	141,192	145,604	150,016	154,428	158,840	163,252	167,663	172,075
15	155,700	160,889	166,079	171,268	176,458	181,648	183,500 *	183,500 *	183,500 *	183,500 *

* Rate limited to the rate for level IV of the Executive Schedule (5 U.S.C. 5304 (g)(1)).

Applicable locations are shown on the 2023 Locality Pay Area Definitions page: http://www.opm.gov/policy-data-oversight/pay-leave/salaries-wages/2023/locality-pay-area-definitions/

(Pictured above: 2023 Salary table for the locality pay area of DC-MD-VA-WV-PA)

In government, we have different "grade levels." While there is an array of positions and pay structures, one of the most common is the General Schedule or GS scale. It starts off at a GS-1 and goes all the way through to a GS-15. Then of course you have the senior executive service and some other areas in government that do pay banding and such things. You'll see the GS-1 through GS-15 scale the most frequently, and it's a good way to help explain this concept a bit more. Say you are getting out of college, and you started off at a GS-5. Looking at OPM's salary table, that's a starting salary of $30K without any modifications based on location... nicely done indeed. But you've been in that role for a year (you're eligible to apply for the next grade level after 52 weeks of service and performing at an acceptable level by the way) and you are now applying for a GS-7 position. You want to be able to show that you have the competencies and the skill sets needed to do the work of a GS-7. It's important to show that you have the established capabilities to ascend to the next level even though you performed the work in a GS-5 position. The same is true across your career as well. Staff need to show they can be a manager. Managers should demonstrate they can be a leader. Leaders should be proven capable of being an executive, and so on. For supervisory positions, show how you've managed teams, projects, activities, and supported personnel activities to show you have the experiences necessary to be a supervisor. Consider the characteristics of a supervisor that you need to have in order to demonstrate that you have the type of experience to really do the work at a higher level. Then, write to that level. It's not just about writing out what you've done, or looking backwards and saying, "Well, you know, maybe it kind of applies." Help the individuals who are doing the evaluations of the resumes or the selecting officials that are actually making the hiring decision. Help them understand that you are the most qualified person for this.

It's a fairly straightforward concept, but we can't tell you how often we've seen applicants miss this when we sit on interview panels or review boards. Candidates may get to the final few but are outpaced by others that have that key set of qualifications they just didn't demonstrate. There's usually only one position that hiring managers are looking to fill so your resume has to help you stand out as the clear choice for the role, not just a top contender.

••• **CONNECT THE DOTS** •••

Speaking of the future, what do you envision to be the next position step in your career journey? Write down a few ideas below.

_____

_____

_____

_____

_____

_____

_____

_____

_____

_____

_____

_____

_____

_____

_____

_____

_____

_____

SHOW THEM YOU CAN PLAY AT THE NEXT LEVEL

It's not just about thinking you can do the work, or "I have some experiences," but really demonstrating that you have the qualifications and the competencies to do that specific type of work. Demonstrate that you really do understand what those requirements are in the first place. This is key to your interview prep as well by the way. For instance, when you're sitting down for an interview, you shouldn't be moving through the motions like you are in a performance review: "Well, here is what I did this past year and here is why I think I am qualified to get this high-level rating." Rather, you should be saying, "Here is what I accomplished and the impact that has been made on the organization as a direct result of my work. This is how I am performing above my grade level and how I believe I am demonstrating my readiness for the next growth level opportunity." In short, you're not just listing activities. You're demonstrating competencies and organizational impact.

If you show hiring and current managers that you have the qualifications and the expertise, it's a whole lot easier for them to determine that you are qualified for the position. If all you are doing is demonstrating that you have already done lower-level stuff, and that's all that you can do, why would they assume that you can do that next level of work? Make sure you are writing and preparing for the future. It's a fantastic reflective exercise and quite possibly the key to your ongoing career growth and fulfillment.

Solving the challenges of higher level work begins with competencies. The person sitting on the other side of the table needs to know that you have the tools necessary to complete these tasks and not the ones you have done already. Many of our clients express some frustration at their job growth. While they are able to perform their duties admirably, there is some question in the minds of their supervisors that they are not ready for the next level. It can be jarring at first but with some reflection and coaching, they can begin to see what they mean. If you find yourself in a similar situation, consider what new actions you can take to perform work outside of your level. Small steps can lead to bigger results. From there, make sure this growth is moving towards the job description of your target job. Before you know it, you'll be demonstrating your readiness for the next level. Plus, even if your current supervisor doesn't see it, you're building your capabilities. If they can't see it, the hiring managers will recognize it in your resume. One way or another, your career growth will be recognized!

In this chapter, we talked about writing for the future to help improve your resume. To recap, there are three things to focus on. How does your experience demonstrate future competency? (1), write to the next grade level (2), and show them that you can play at that next level (3). It's important to show them that you know exactly what to do and how to get things done... because you've done it before.

Now, go get 'em, tiger!

••• **CONNECT THE DOTS** •••

Are you ready for career growth? Take a moment to write down one strategy you plan to use to show you can play at the next level.

_____

_____

_____

_____

_____

_____

_____

_____

_____

_____

_____

_____

_____

_____

_____

_____

_____

NOTES AND REFLECTIONS

Consider the strategies in this chapter. What new insight do you have that you didn't have before? How will you use this in your resume?

_____

_____

_____

_____

_____

_____

_____

What "next level" job requirements are in store for you? What can you do now to prepare for them?

_____

_____

_____

_____

_____

_____

_____

How do you plan to demonstrate you're ready for the next level?

_____

_____

_____

_____

_____

_____

_____

INSIDER'S TIP

Ready to make a difference in the lives of your colleagues and the world? That's what effective leaders do at every level in government. Supervisory and non-supervisory alike, we each can manage our work to help transform the world around us. As you write your resume, you may find it helpful to connect your experiences to how you have made an impact on those around you. Demonstrate you're good to work with, for, and around. As you do so, you'll be demonstrating how you are a good fit for the role now and in the future.

Patrick R. Leddin and Shawn D. Moon get right to the heart of this in their book *Building a winning culture in government.* Their chapter on building effective leaders at every leader especially hits home for us. Take a look at their book and consider how your work now is setting up a culture for strong performance tomorrow. Writing that in your resume is a solid strategy to capture your leadership credentials!

Leddin, P. R., Moon, S. D., & Leddin, P. (2018). *Building a winning culture in government: A blueprint for delivering success in the public sector* (1st ed.). Mango Media.

CHAPTER 8:

CONNECT WITH WHAT YOU ENJOY

This is an often-overlooked concept in career management. We have bills, requirements, and family obligations whose importance crowds out the meaningful. The idea that you set aside what you love in order to do what you have to do for your greater responsibilities. You may have some lingering thoughts from your parents as you were growing up on this topic. You may be reading this book because you are in a spot and really need that next job. All of this can still be true, but here's the thing… What if you could have both?

We're really excited about this chapter because it is the most meaningful and most impactful. What can be better than meeting all your financial obligations by pursuing meaningful work that you enjoy? As Theodore Roosevelt reminds us: "Far and away the best prize that life has to offer is the chance to work hard at work worth doing." Public service is not only worthwhile as a means of serving others it can be a source of professional enjoyment as well.

So, the main strategy is, connect with what you enjoy. Why is this important? We all want to have a degree of happiness and fulfillment in our work. Think about it. Do you want to go to a job that you really don't like doing? Do you want to be doing work that you find boring or frustrating? Probably not. If you are curious about how you can get a full-time, great paying job that connects with what you enjoy, this chapter is for you.

We have three strategies for us to discuss in this chapter. First, align your joys with their needs. Number two, ask yourself "What is it that I want to do more of?" And lastly, number three, picture what brings you joy.

TOPICS COVERED:
* Align your joys with your needs
* Ask yourself "What do I want to do more of?"
* Picture what brings you joy

ALIGN YOUR JOYS WITH THEIR NEEDS

If you can find things that you really like doing, and then allow yourself to find where that joy is in your work, you will have a great time and find a lot of happiness. The whole idea is trying to figure out what it is that you enjoy and what it is that they need (your job requirements).

We each have things that bring us happiness but have you ever wondered what about those activities makes you happy? Think about that for a moment. What is it about the little things that get your blood pumping? Is it the excitement at learning something new or the heart-warming feeling of helping someone else. It could even be the thrill of solving the unsolvable...

Here's a great example: Karen, our fellow Gov Geek, really enjoys puzzles. She likes mysteries, she likes novels, she likes all these great things where she gets to uncover the answer (you should see how wrapped up she gets in these!). Amazingly enough, one of the great things that she does in her job is (drum roll please) solving puzzles. Now, what does this really mean? Well, she recognized a valuable component of her work was data analysis. From excel spreadsheets and financial systems to contracts and personnel forecasting, she tries to figure out root causes for concerns or issues. They are the puzzles her leadership needs worked out and a source of workplace fulfillment for her. She chooses to see it as a big puzzle that she gets to solve. That's part of what really brings about a lot of joy for her. These are simply the things that she really likes to do.

So, for you to align your joy with their needs, think about the organization. What is it that the work is doing? Are they solving puzzles? Are they interacting with people? Research the organization and, if possible, speak with those in your network that work there to find the organization's needs. Then, consider what really interests you? How can you use what you've learned or even just the job requirements given to you to find joy? When you can focus on that, there you go! That's where a lot of the happiness is. Your career satisfaction may be closer than you think once you find a workplace that aligns with your passions.

••• CONNECT THE DOTS •••

Where do you find joy in your work? What about hobbies? Outline a few projects or activities below along with how they can prepare you for this new role.

_____

_____

_____

_____

_____

_____

_____

_____

_____

_____

_____

_____

_____

_____

_____

_____

_____

_____

_____

ASK YOURSELF "WHAT DO I WANT TO DO MORE OF?"

Take a second and think about where you have been in your career. If you have been in one position for a great many years, or even just a few weeks, ask yourself: What are the times that you really found happiness? What are the projects that you really remember bringing you joy? What are the assignments that really lit you up, made you glow with happiness, pride, and a sense of accomplishment and you recall wanting to have more of that? If this is your first job, well then think about what it is that you have always liked to do? What are some things that you can honestly just spend hours doing, and not even realize it? The time just kind of flies by and you find yourself wondering what happened to the day. When you can be really honest with yourself about what particular things you really enjoy, then you can ask yourself how you can find a way to do more of that. This will help you begin to understand how to say yes to the things that you enjoy and grow away from the things that you don't.

The more of a clear understanding you have of this joy-creating line of work, the easier it is for you to really project that joy in the job interview and during the job as a 9 to 5. It also helps you to seek out like-minded people through networking and find the positions that are suited to your unique kind of joy. This is career fulfillment. The alternative is a bit more bleak. You don't want to be sitting there thinking, "Oh my gosh, it's barely Monday afternoon and I have to go through the whole week in order for it to finally be the weekend." That's not really a great way to live. So, ask yourself really and truly, what is it that you want to do more of?

PHOTO CREDIT to Success Pictures

Here's a great example of the weekly grind. Notice the struggle of Monday and the joy of Saturday. Is this the kind of work you're used to? If the anxiety of Sunday evening is greater than the joy of Friday afternoon, you may be in the wrong opportunity. Working in public service means there are plenty of positions to choose from. There just may be that ideal position for you out there!

••• **CONNECT THE DOTS** •••

After looking at the above illustration, think about what worries you about Sunday afternoons. What aspect of the fear about Monday morning resonates with you?

_____

_____

_____

_____

_____

_____

_____

_____

_____

_____

_____

_____

_____

_____

_____

_____

_____

_____

_____

_____

PICTURE WHAT BRINGS YOU JOY

If you close your eyes, can you visualize the type of project or the activity that you like? It doesn't necessarily have to be the ultimate be all and end all thing that will be the perfect job, but more what are the things that you just like doing? What kind of activity brings you happiness? You might have a nice chuckle and think, "What brings me joy is to not work at all!" or, "I just enjoy spending time with my family." It's totally acceptable to have that thought. We each have an idea of what work is and is not. Plus, our picture of enjoyment is different as well. Consider what sorts of activities bring you joy outside of your 9 to 5. If you enjoy time with family, what are the sorts of activities you enjoy together? Take the time to consider the activities that spark some joy in your life. If you feel you have to work, wouldn't it be great to work on something you actually want to do?

Here's an exercise to help you visualize a possible career path for yourself: If you were to look forward into the future, and you could think to yourself, "If I could be doing this project or activity for an extended period of time, how happy would I be?" Or, can you identify what you are really curious about and would like to explore? When you can picture yourself spending a lot of time doing something you enjoy, you'll have the beginning of something great. It's kind of like one of those career questions that you no doubt had earlier on in life. Perhaps even in high school when you were talking to your guidance counselor, and they asked you what you'd do with a million dollars and didn't need to work at all. The purpose of the question was to give you the opportunity to really think: if you didn't have to worry about money, what would you like to do? Some people want to be videographers, while others want to be communications experts. Other people really enjoy medicine or the law. And if they can really lose themselves in that type of work, then at the end of the day, it's not work at all because you are enjoying everything that you are doing. The goal shouldn't be to have lots of money or buy lots of things (as awesome as that sounds), it should be to think of what activity speaks to you.

Also, if you're having some challenges finding what that is for you, you may be well served by exploring some options. Use YouTube videos, Facebook groups, TikTok accounts, and other easily accessible platforms to search for topics of interest. Speak with friends, colleagues, relatives, and others about different options as well. Become a sponge to find what interests you. The bigger picture to avoid is postponing your dreams for a later date like retirement to finally do the things that make you happy.

On a bit of a serious note here, we don't have unlimited time available to us. We may think of tomorrow as a guaranteed option, but it's really not. We've known some terrific friends and colleagues who were happy to finally retire so they could do what they have always wanted to do. They decided to delay their happiness for retirement instead of embracing it as a core function of their lives. Unfortunately some passed away within a year or so of leaving work. We share this not to frighten you but to help shed some light on why all of this really matters. To have so many hopes and dreams in your hands when your time is up is no way to say your farewells. What you do matters not only for others but also for yourself. We truly hope you find the joy you're looking for as soon as you can!

In this chapter we spoke a little bit about how you can connect with what you enjoy in writing your resumes. We looked at three important things. First off, what is it that aligns your joys with their needs? With the organization's needs, the hiring manager's needs, etcetera. Number two, what do you want to do more of? Really being honest with yourself and asking what is it that I could spend hours doing and just be happy doing that at work? And lastly, number three, picture what brings you joy. Picture the things that you can really find a lot of enjoyment in, now and in the future.

When you combine all of these together, you are connecting with items that really bring you joy. And when you are placing that in your resume, it connects with what you enjoy and therefore connects with the individuals that are looking for that very same thing because they are looking to hire a person that really enjoys that type of work (mind-blown!). That's why they're hiring for that position. They want to know the person will be engaged, productive, and easy to work with. If you love your work, odds are you'll be just the right person they're looking for.

So, heck, go out there and find your happiness!

••• **CONNECT THE DOTS** •••

Think of the activities you genuinely look forward to doing. What about them makes them fun for you? How will this next job help bring you closer to that feeling?

_____

_____

_____

_____

_____

_____

_____

_____

_____

_____

_____

_____

_____

_____

_____

_____

_____

_____

NOTES AND REFLECTIONS

Looking at the jobs you're targeting, what about the work do you find fun?

_____

_____

_____

_____

_____

_____

_____

How do you know you'll enjoy this work? How could you find out more?

_____

_____

_____

_____

_____

_____

_____

What can you do to avoid that "Sunday evening feeling"?

_____

_____

_____

_____

_____

_____

_____

INSIDER'S TIP

Did you find it a challenge to describe what brings you joy in your work? If so, you're not alone. Our clients and colleagues have expressed to us that they don't look to their job for joy or fulfillment. Instead they find themselves grinding through the workday for the paycheck then take the commute home to unwind before starting it up again. We're here to say that there is another way. Finding joy in your work should be a goal in your job hunt. Why not work in a position that helps you feel energetic and useful? It may not sound possible and we realize we only covered a bit of that in this book. Until we capture this in greater detail as we've learned it, we're happy to recommend another resource that has helped us.

Celebrated author and speaker Shawn Achor explains how you can be more productive, creative, and better problem solvers with happiness. His book, *The Happiness Advantage: How a Positive Brain Fuels Success in Work and Life*, may just be the resource you need to create the joy you've been searching for!

Achor, S. (2010). *The happiness advantage* (3rd ed.). Random House Digital Inc.

CHAPTER 9:

USE GSA TO YOUR ADVANTAGE

Ahh GSA Advantage. If you've had the chance to use it before, you know how impressive this system is. Think of Amazon.com for Government services and products. A central place where you can find just about everything. GSA Advantage (pictured below) is an online government purchasing service run by the General Services Administration (GSA). So, why is this good for your resume? In short, it describes what the Government wants and how much they are willing to pay for it. It's a terrific strategy to align your career passions with their needs. In this chapter, we'll talk more about using GSA Advantage.

TOPICS COVERED:

- What is GSA Advantage?
- Search services by job title
- Use GSA Advantage to research position qualifications
- Use the salaries

WHAT IS GSA ADVANTAGE?

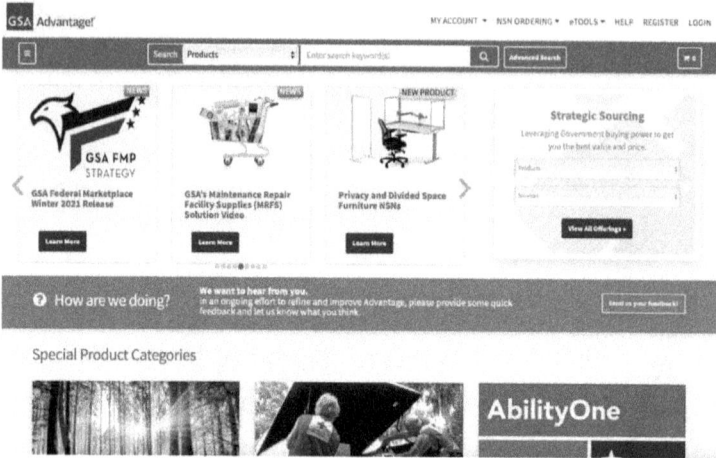

GSA Advantage! is an online shopping and ordering system providing access to thousands of contractors and millions of products and services (US General Services Administration [GSA]). The Administration focused this website on federal staff who are searching for products and services from vendors who have been vetted by GSA. GSA has already negotiated rates and costs so the employee doesn't have to, plus the employee can purchase the goods using a GSA schedule contract so, again, they don't have to go through that long process on their own. As you can see, this service is very useful. You go to the site, choose if it's a service, a product, or a supply, type into the search bar, and then you find the organizations that do that type of work. Having used it before, we can attest to how helpful this is to avoid general bureaucracies when ordering office supplies (but that's another book entirely!).

Why is GSA Advantage such a great thing for resume writing? Let me tell you. It's fantastic because it describes the skills, the qualifications, and the pay rates for the individuals that do that work. So, quite simply, you can go to GSA Advantage, type in whatever your job title is, find the agencies or organizations that are looking to hire for that type of work or the companies that are selling that type of work. And from there, find tons of resources and information on where the work is and how much the government is willing to pay for it. You can see how a person is qualified or not qualified for a certain level (entry, mid-career, executive, etc.) and how much typically the government pays for those services.

SEARCH SERVICES BY JOB TITLE

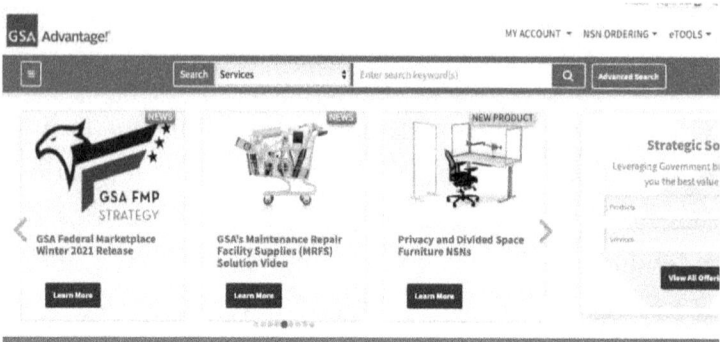

All right then. Let's dive into how to use it. At the very top in the search bar, there is a little dropdown box, click that, and then go to the services area and type in your job title (see Chapter 8 to find job titles that bring you joy). Once you hit search, you are going to get a ton of organizations and companies that provide those services to the government. From there, you can simply click directly onto the name of these organizations and pull up their GSA negotiated contract. The companies have already gone through the process of working directly with GSA to say these are the types of services, this is the cost, and this is the value that the government is getting.

In the company document, you can see what the educational requirements are, how much the rates are for those different positions, and really, why those types of jobs exist. You know - what the main goals or objectives are for them. As you are looking at this, you can begin to do a bit of an analysis. You can ask yourself, "What skill set should a person have to be qualified to do this work, and do I have those qualifications?" Degrees, years of experiences, skill sets, certifications, and more. These items can give you a better sense of determining if you have the qualifications necessary for that position. Plus, you can see what the organizations are charging for your work to see if they are paying you well enough. This kind of market research is critical to know how eager the market is to pay for your qualifications. Talk about empowerment!

••• **CONNECT THE DOTS** •••

Let's look at the website. Search for services related to your career goals. What organizations do you feel align with you? What positions do you see a connection with your qualifications?

_____

_____

_____

_____

_____

_____

_____

_____

_____

_____

_____

_____

_____

_____

_____

_____

USE GSA ADVANTAGE TO RESEARCH POSITION QUALIFICATIONS

We covered a little bit about looking at the types of experiences and degrees, but you can use this resource to think about the bigger set of qualifications needed for your career growth. This is wonderful for career planning. For instance, if you know what you love to do and you don't need a graduate degree (or several) to do it – should you decide to get into debt to finance your graduate education? In another instance, if you need to have more specialized experience, are there other areas you can find this expertise such as detail positions, volunteer opportunities, or even short-term projects? This is like a crystal ball to help you prepare for the future. Imagine how great it would be to save yourself tens of thousands of dollars in tuition (yup, we've been there too) or build the ideal skills needed for your dream career while others are still figuring it all out. Knowledge is indeed power, my friends!

As you consider what you don't need for your ideal career, take the time to see what really is in value. The companies listed on this site have an "Authorized Federal Supply Schedule Price List" that describes the GSA approved pricing and descriptions - including qualifications and requirements for each service area or labor category they offer. From degrees and certifications to years of experience and professional association memberships, this information lays out what is valued by government agencies. As you read this, decide what you should emphasize in your resume. What are the areas that you have been undervaluing or not including in your resume? If there are areas you don't have well-established, what steps can you take to strengthen those areas? These are meaningful questions to ask yourself because they can guide you to your bigger career picture.

Next, take a look at job announcements for your target position and compare them with the capabilities described in GSA Advantage. Notice how much an individual earns for this type of work and the qualifications that are necessary. Compare those qualifications and yours, then consider if you meet the requirements necessary to do the work. As career coaches, we have seen many of our clients realize that they are not only qualified for their dream jobs, but are also not getting paid enough in their current job! Then there's a sort of rush of confidence because the proof of their qualifications is right there in front of them. They can see what the work is, recognize their compatibility, and feel empowered to make their dreams a reality and apply. I mean, why wouldn't they?

If you are writing to the job duties and the qualifications in the GSA advantage documents as well as applying the other lessons you've learned in this book because you see how your qualifications stand up against the standards, why shouldn't you expect the same success? This strategy helps you demonstrate that you have all the qualifications necessary. If agencies are using the job announcements and GSA Advantage to describe what they are looking for, it just makes sense to write to those qualifications. It's like having the answers to the test. There's a strong expectation that you can be referred for that position if you demonstrate the qualifications they're looking for in a candidate.

At the risk of sounding like an infomercial... but that's not all! This is a great way to see if you are writing to the requirements correctly. If you feel you've written your resume well enough but aren't getting referrals or interviews, then you might want to take a step back and think to yourself, "Okay, am I writing to them appropriately? What am I missing? What are some of the things that I can do better?" You know, often as we are working with clients, they will tell us certain things like, "Oh gosh, you know, I can't tell you how many jobs I have applied for, but I never hear back," or, "I have been on so many interviews, but unfortunately, I never get called in for the second interview, or I never actually get offered the job."

Here's a great way to find out why. If you find yourself in a similar position, you now have the means to go back and see if there's something you can do about it.

That alone is a relief for many people. At least they can finally understand what they need to do better to improve their chances at landing in the career field they're aiming for. It can be a whole lot easier to feel frustrated about the process or even down on yourself about where you are in your career search. But this is one of the many tools that you can use to find out if your qualifications are really coming through in your resume. Using this strategy, you'll know how to make some tweaks to help your resume really get seen by hiring managers in a way that matters.

••• CONNECT THE DOTS •••

While on the site and looking at a few of the federal supply schedule price lists, what qualifications do you still need to feel qualified for your target role? What aspect of the qualifications do you feel you already have enough experience?

_____

_____

_____

_____

_____

_____

_____

_____

_____

_____

_____

_____

_____

_____

_____

_____

_____

_____

USE THE SALARIES

The third and final tip on using GSA Advantage is probably one of the most fun ones; use the salaries. If the government is willing to pay for the services at a certain rate, then you also look at the positions that people are hiring for on GSA Advantage and you see the salary ranges that are listed there, it's easy for you to understand salary expectations for yourself. You'll know just how much you should expect for that work. It's a really wonderful planning tool. Say you have found what you really love and realize the amount of money you'll earn isn't amazingly high, you can make an informed decision as you get into the field. Alternatively, you can opt for another line of work that meets your financial requirements with the knowledge that you won't enjoy it as much as the work you really love. Either way, you can make an informed decision about your future. The information is there for you to become empowered.

For instance, when you have submitted a brilliant resume (using the remarkable insights in this book, of course) and have completed all the interviews needed to be offered a wonderful job; how much should you expect in salary? The human capital team will offer you a base salary but is that the right amount? Perhaps a signing bonus or other incentive would be appropriate? Using this market research, you could go back and politely mention that a 5% increase to a higher step, more benefits such as a tuition reimbursement, or some other incentive would be appropriate for you. You'll know, based upon the research that you have done, how much money is reasonable for you to earn in that position. This is especially great if you are working outside of government and you want to get a job in government. You could say, "Okay, well, I know that based on market research that they pay this amount for this type of service or type of skill set." So, if they are paying that to others, why aren't they paying you that? Why isn't that something that you should look for?

After reading all of this, aren't you glad you know more about GSA Advantage? At first glance, it's easy to question the relationship. Once you see the connection and how it can truly serve you, it's tough to miss!

In this chapter we looked at search characteristics of the site (job titles, salary expectations, etc.). Second, we covered how you can use the site to research position qualifications for career planning. Lastly, we covered using GSA Advantage to manage salary expectations. In each phase, you learned how having access to a proven and continuously updated system is awesome for your career.

As a closing thought, this strategy is incredible but just the tip of the proverbial career iceberg. Take the time to consider other websites and materials that may be of use to you in your career. We have seen funds and access to other benefits suddenly materialize when presented with the right need. The more aware you are of your value and the market's willingness to pay for your services, the more equipped you'll be for the job and your long-term job satisfaction. Use these insights to build a career that you love so that your work can benefit the lives of those we serve as public servants. You've got this!

••• CONNECT THE DOTS •••

A popular topic to be sure, what do you feel your salary expectations should be based on what you're seeing?

_____

_____

_____

_____

_____

_____

_____

_____

_____

_____

_____

_____

_____

_____

_____

_____

_____

_____

_____

_____

_____

NOTES AND REFLECTIONS

What qualifications did you find in your GSA Advantage search?

_____

_____

_____

_____

_____

_____

Looking at the rates, what range should you expect your salary to be?

_____

_____

_____

_____

_____

_____

This is one data point for your job market search. Where else could you find more?

_____

_____

_____

_____

_____

_____

_____

INSIDER'S TIP

This chapter has been all about market research using GSA Advantage. While this resource is tremendous, we recognize that it is not all that is out there. No doubt you have looked into LinkedIn already as well. While you can find an array of federal government opportunities there you may also benefit from conducting some market research while you're there as well. Take a look at salaries, job descriptions, trends of qualifications people have in roles you're interested in occupying. All of it is there for the taking. It's also worth taking a deeper dive into some strategies to make the most of your efforts.

Linked: Conquer LinkedIn. Get Your Dream Job. Own Your Future is a book that can help you to do just that. Learn more about networking, building your brand, and leveraging all that glorious data to help you build your resume and accelerate your career outlook. Applying even a few of the techniques can help you refine your approach. Every little step is worth it!

Garriott, O., & Schifeling, J. (2022). *Linked: Conquer linkedin. get your dream job. own your future.* Workman Publishing Company.

REFERENCES

ABOUT THIS BOOK

Dewey, J. (1933). *How we think: A restatement of the relation of reflective thinking to the educative process.* Henry Regency.

CHAPTER 1

Tolver, K. (2020). *Career rehab: Rebuild your personal brand and rethink the way you work.* Entrepreneur Press.

CHAPTER 2

Partnership for Public Service. (n.d.). *Tools.* Public service leadership institute. Retrieved March 10, 2023, from https://ourpublicservice.org/public-service-leadership-institute/tools.

CHAPTER 3

Falcone, P. (2005). *2600 phrases for effective performance reviews: Ready-to-use words and phrases that really get results* (39256th ed.). AMACOM.

CHAPTER 4

Both-Nwabuwe, J. C., Dijkstra, M. M., & Beersma, B. (2017). Sweeping the floor or putting a man on the moon:

How to define and measure meaningful work. Frontiers in Psychology, 8. https://doi.org/10.3389/fpsyg.2017.01658

Daly, P. H., Watkins, M., & Reavis, C. (2006). *The first 90 days in government: Critical success strategies for new public managers at all levels* (1st ed.). Harvard Business Review Press.

CHAPTER 5

Neral, J. (2020). *Show up: Six strategies to lead a more energetic and impactful career.* John Neral Coaching.

CHAPTER 6

Spatola, M. (2023). *The office is dead, now what?: A pos-pandemic field guide for leadership.* New Degree Press.

US Office of Personnel Management. (n.d.-a). About. Retrieved March 12, 2023, from https://www.opm.gov /about-us.

US Office of Personnel Management. (n.d.). *Classifying general schedule positions.* Retrieved March 12, 2023, from https://www.opm.gov/policy-data-oversight/classi-fication-qualifications/classifying-general--schedule-positions

CHAPTER 7

Leddin, P. R., Moon, S. D., & Leddin, P. (2018). *Building a winning culture in government: A blueprint for delivering success in the public sector* (1st ed.). Mango Media.

US Office of Personnel Management. (n.d.-c). *Salary table 2023-DCB*. Retrieved March 12, 2023, from https://www.opm.gov/policy-data-oversight/pay-leave/salaries-wages/salary-tables/pdf/2023/DCB.pdf

CHAPTER 8

Achor, S. (2010). *The happiness advantage* (3rd ed.). Random House Digital Inc.

Success Pictures. (n.d.). Retrieved March 12, 2023, from https://successpictures.io

CHAPTER 9

Garriott, O., & Schifeling, J. (2022). *Linked: Conquer linkedin. get your dream job. own your future.* Workman Publishing Company.

US General Services Administration. (n.d.). *How to buy through us*. Retrieved March 12, 2023, from https://www.gsa.gov/buy-through-us/new-to-gsa-acquisitions/how-to-buy-through-us

RESOURCES FROM THE GOV GEEKS

As well as coaching and training services, we also provide free learning material about various aspects of career management. These resources include templates, self-paced learning components, podcasts, live shows, and videos. To learn more, check out our events tab on TheGovGeeks.com!

RESUME TEMPLATES

Sign up for the *GovGeekdom* – The Gov Geeks community of your fellow public servants - to receive: *"Launching your purpose-driven career... How to craft a government resume."* A video training program with free templates and resources! Learn how to craft a government resume that exceeds applicant tracking systems, human capital experts, and hiring manager requirements.

GOV GEEKS ASSEMBLE!

G*Gov Geeks Assemble!* is a podcast like only The Gov Geeks could offer! Career tools, interviews, and other awesomeness. Level up your 9 to 5 on 95 by listening on YouTube, your favorite podcast platform... or right from our website! Fun, engaging, and packed with solid support, don't be surprised if you end up binging these shows!

TICKETED MASTERCLASS EVENTS

Join us for 60-minute, limited registration-only events focused on career, professional, and management development in government. Engage The Gov Geeks themselves in meaningful discussions about your work, career aspirations, and how to truly find purpose in your work - all in a live setting! Attendees depart with actionable strategies and tools to implement in their lives to drive their career and organizational change.

LINKEDIN SERIES

High-impact and short professional development videos are posted on LinkedIn for your ease of access and convenience. Each nine-part series ranges from resumes and interviews to soft skill management and career planning, with new topics constantly added. Get what you need to get your career and agency going!

VIDEO LIBRARY

Watch our shows live on TheGovGeeks.com, LinkedIn, or YouTube! Crashing on a deadline or interested in other videos? No worries! Check out our interviews, shows, tutorials, and fun career management content in our career development library. Learn at your pace and have fun along the way. Seriously… go check it out!

COACHING CONSULTATIONS

Sign up to explore your goals and see how coaching can help you bring your vision to life! A free thirty-minute consultation gives you the opportunity to see if coaching would be of value to you and if we are the right fit for you. We're pretty awesome but know it's all about fit. We're here to support you wherever your journey takes you. A thirty-minute investment can lead to life-changing results!

ABOUT THE GOV GEEKS, LLC

We provide coaching and training services for the government to help public servants achieve meaningful fulfillment and serve the American people. From executive and career coaching to professional and management development training, we're on a mission to help you find fulfillment in public service.

After serving nearly 40 years in public service in roles ranging from entry-level to the executive suite, we know the unique challenges of working within the federal government... but we also know the value. Civil servants have the opportunity to make a real difference in the world. We aim to help you live a fulfilling life. The way we see it, the public benefits when you are able to perform at your best. Trust The Gov Geeks to help you make the most of your time in public service - for you and for our nation.

FOLLOW US ON SOCIAL MEDIA!
LinkedIn: linkedin.com/company/the-gov-geeks
YouTube: youtube.com/thegovgeeks
Instagram: instagram.com/thegovgeeks

Scan this QR code to stay connected with your friendly neighborhood Gov Geeks!

ABOUT THE GOV GEEKS THEMSELVES

Javier Lopez, MSA, PCC - Javier proudly serves as the Geek in Chief and Co-Founder of The Gov Geeks LLC, a learning and professional development endeavor committed to helping public servants get in and get ahead in government. Through coaching, workshop facilitation, and public addresses, Javier presents the genuine value of service.

Drawing upon over two decades as a high-performing federal executive and an Adjunct Professor of organizational leadership, Javier is a scholar-practitioner and keynote speaker who offers helpful career strategies that focus on personal empowerment and mission success. His unique insights are of value to individuals and organizations alike.

Javier was born in El Paso, Texas. He holds a Master of Science in Administration from Trinity Washington University and a Bachelor of Arts from the University of Texas at El Paso. He is credentialed as a Professional Certified Coach (PCC) from the International Coaching Federation (ICF) and a Certified Professional Coach (CPC) from the Institute of Professional Excellence in Coaching (iPEC). Equipped with an array of professional training and certifications, he is well-versed in the functions of government. Javier is committed to using his experience, training, and energy to fulfill the potential of others.

He is happily married to a fellow gov geek, grateful for two wonderful daughters, and resides in Alexandria, Virginia. A full-time public servant himself, his work with The Gov Geeks is not part of any official duties or responsibilities.

FOLLOW JAVIER ON SOCIAL MEDIA!
LinkedIn: linkedin.com/in/javierlopezmsa
Instagram: instagram.com/geek_in_chief

Karen Lopez, BS - Karen is the Co-Founder and Executive Director of The Gov Geeks, LLC. A native Texan with a passion for public service, she combines her love of science and human behavior to successfully implement programs within the Federal Government. Her expertise spans across human resource management and organizational leadership to curriculum development and financial operations.

Drawing upon over 20 years of progressively expanding responsibility evaluating and directing programs as a federal executive, Karen takes joy in mentoring others and being of value to the mission of any organization lucky enough to work with her. From supporting cognitive brain research at the University of Texas at El Paso with the Department of Defense (DoD) to improving diplomatic functions at the Department of State, Mrs. Lopez has made a true difference for the nation.

Karen holds a B.S. in Human Resource Management from Trinity Washington University and a graduate certificate from American University's Key Leadership Program. While Mrs. Lopez has proven to be driven and capable, she humbly admits she cannot take full credit for her accomplishments. Her successes are a direct result of partnerships with those she works with and the constant support of her husband and two daughters. As a

THE GOV GEEKS | JAVIER AND KAREN LOPEZ

full-time public servant, her work with The Gov Geeks is not part of any official duties or responsibilities.

FOLLOW KAREN ON SOCIAL MEDIA!

LinkedIn: linkedin.com/in/lopezkaren
Instagram: instagram.com/thechicgovgeek

204

SERVICES FROM THE GOV GEEKS

CAREER COACHING

How are you going to stand out to government recruiters and hiring officials? Partner with The Gov Geeks to build a career strategy that showcases the value of your experience, competencies, and career purpose. More than cookie-cutter resumes that get lost among other applications, the right approach can position you as the clear choice for selecting officials in the federal government.

Find your purpose with our career coaching services. Each component is a step toward unlocking fulfilling work in government - not just another job.

Whether you are a recent graduate, working professional, experienced leader, or senior executive, we will partner with you to craft an impactful resume that meets your career aspirations and the government's needs. More than a cut-and-paste resume shop, The Gov Geeks takes care to work with you to align what drives you and what agencies need.

EXECUTIVE COACHING

Enhance your career and agency by developing leadership skills, finding fulfillment in your work, or supporting your team. From searching for your next position to a complete career change, our certified coaches will work with you one-on-one to identify your strengths, and opportunities, and create an action plan to reach your goals!

We are experts in executive coaching and believe in the important role you play in government. We want you to reach your full potential so that the public receives the best services possible. It is our priority to help you achieve success in your career today and in the future!

TRAINING SERVICES

Trust The Gov Geeks to offer training services that empower your team to reach their full potential. With specialties across fields such as career transitions, communication skills development, team building, and leadership, you're sure to find topics that will support your organization.

All our presentations are developed in a modular format which allows us to offer you custom-tailored solutions. Designed as a one-day (8-hour) course, each can be reduced or expanded in length to meet your specific needs, including keynote speeches and seminars. Each course includes highly experiential sessions that build both knowledge and practical skills. We are also available to provide our training courses as a series of interactive webinars. As an alternative, The Gov Geeks also provides custom eLearning and blended learning programs.

KEYNOTE SPEECHES

Book the speaker who nails it! When the perfect speaker steps in front of the right audience, organizations and individuals can solve their toughest challenges and improve in lasting ways. Consider hiring a trusted expert for your virtual meeting, conference, corporate event, seminar, trade show, convention, or workshop. We're proud to be of support to you and your attendees!

OTHER BOOKS FROM THE GOV GEEKS

THE GOV GEEKS GUIDE TO GOVERNMENT NETWORKING

Are you looking for career advancement opportunities but finding the idea of networking to be a challenge?

Are you looking for a way to build meaningful partnerships in your career but don't feel like you have the time, resources, or way to go about it?

Networking brings up thoughts of some unsavory experiences for many people. The idea of going to crowded events and conferences, having forced conversations with strangers, exchanging business cards, or searching for exclusive conversations with influential people who can create job opportunities with just a simple phone call seems like the norm. But it doesn't have to be. If this is your only perspective of networking, you're not alone. In fact, it is quite common to misinterpret what quality networking actually looks like. If only there was another way!

The Gov Geeks Guide to Networking is a wonderful resource to help you through these misconceptions. With practical and actionable strategies, this guide can help change your life immeasurably. Give yourself the opportunity to consider a new approach that values your strengths and nurtures your relationships.

Javier and Karen bring over 40 years of federal career experience building sustainable professional relationships to this book. Leveraging countless partnerships with executives and influential career public servants, this book gathers their insights in an easy-to-understand and fun way.

Networking is about finding common ground through supportive relationships, not shortcuts that take advantage of others. If you're looking for proven techniques to support your professional and aspirational goals, you'll find yourself referring back to this guide time and again!

THE GOV GEEKS GUIDE TO GOVERNMENT JOB INTERVIEWS

Do you find job interviews for the federal government to be a challenge?

Does the idea about being put on the spot and evaluated by strangers weird you out?

Well, it's only natural to feel that way! **Job interviews** can be challenging. As tense of a scenario as you can imagine, sitting across from another individual or panel of individuals to be deemed qualified can be one of the most tense times in your life. Plus, it's not like you get to go through this experience every day to help make sure you are comfortable and prepared. As challenging as this sounds, there is a way forward!

The Gov Geeks Guide to Job Interviews was designed by two Federal employees with over 40 years of government experience between them and dozens of interviews on both sides of the table. We know the challenges and the opportunities first-hand add a reminder to share valuable insights to help you crush the interview and find fulfillment in a government career. From insights with human capital experts and discussions with Chief Human Capital Officers to first-hand experiences as both candidates and selecting officials, this book will give you a competitive edge in your career search.

From entry through executive levels, if you are looking to make a wise investment in your career advancement and learn life-changing job interview strategies, this is the book for you!

THE GOV GEEKS GUIDE TO GOVERNMENT SOFT SKILLS

Have you found the secret element to landing the perfect job or being promoted?

What about meaningful tools to manage your career outside of all the technical skills you've developed?

From entry to executive levels, **soft skills** are a key component of career development. They're those non-technical skills that enable you to work with others. Beyond degrees, certifications, years of experience, and other credentials, these attributes can determine how far you can advance in your career or whether you'll have the opportunity to begin the job in the first place. Learning how to foster and apply them to your career is fundamental for growth and success.

The Gov Geeks Guide to Soft Skills is your hands-on resource to empower you with tested and actionable strategies to manage your career in the federal government.

After building their careers across 40 years of public service to executive roles, Javier and Karen understand the need for strong soft skills. The Gov Geeks themselves want to share their hard-won insights to help you manage your opportunities and find professional fulfillment in your work.

If you're looking for tools to build a rewarding and expansive career in the federal government, this book is for you!

ABOUT THE PUBLISHER

Dear Reader,

Thank you for purchasing this unique book and joining the Live Life Happy Community of readers. We are a publishing company committed to bringing positive, supportive, and well-being-enhancing books to life.

We offer a hybrid approach to bringing books to life at *Live Life Happy Publishing*. We specialize in helping exceptional individuals share their knowledge, expertise and experience with the world.

We believe nothing should hold accomplished individuals back from spreading their word. We also believe authors deserve 100% of the royalties for their hard-earned knowledge, effort and desire to support humanity. We have reinvented the publishing industry with our hybrid publishing model.

Live Life Happy Publishing was birthed out of necessity and is more aligned with the current publishing landscape. To serve a unique community devoted to enhancing lives and bridging the gap between self-publishing and traditional publishing, we pride ourselves on bringing titles to market fast with worldwide distribution in all formats.

Are you an aspiring author and have a book in your heart? Let us help share the powerful message and bring your book to life!

Books Change Lives: Whose life will you touch with yours? Reach out for a personal approach to book writing and publishing.

Live Life Happy Publishing: Your Hybrid approach to bringing your book to life!

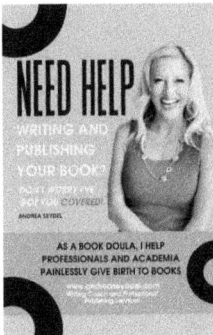

Andrea Seydel (The Book Doula)
Founder of *Live Life Happy Publishing*
www.livelifehappypublishing.com

www.ingramcontent.com/pod-product-compliance
Lightning Source LLC
Chambersburg PA
CBHW031809190326
41518CB00006B/263